Policing the Underworld

Policing the Underworld

The Life of San Francisco Detective Arthur McQuaide in the Golden Age of Vice & Violence

To Frank & Sharon,
I hope you enjoy this true story of an honorable California lawman!

Cheyenne, WY
2019

By Erik J. Wright

Foreword by Samuel K. Dolan

Tripaw Press

© All Rights Reserved under the author and Tripaw Press.

ISBN-13: 978-1986702652

ISBN-10: 1986702650

Paperback, First Edition. Printed in the United States of America

No part of this written and copyrighted work may be reproduced electronically or by any other means without the express written consent of the author and/or publisher.

Det. Arthur McQuaide, San Francisco Police Department, circa 1920.
Courtesy San Francisco Public Library.

FOR CHRIS BUNCH, PARAGOULD POLICE DEPARTMENT

...Lawman, family man, friend to all.

contents

Maps
Introduction
Acknowledgements
Foreword by Samuel K. Dolan
Prologue

Chapter 1 – Cauldron of Violence ... 1
Chapter 2 – California or Bust ... 8
Chapter 3 – Rookie ... 13

Photos

Chapter 4 – Big Trouble in Little China ... 20
Chapter 5 – Lost Years ... 24
Chapter 6 – The Horrible Dream of 1906 ... 26

Photos

Chapter 7 – Arkansas Fugitive ... 33
Chapter 8 – Well-Known to Thousands ... 42

Appendix I ... 46
Appendix II ... 79
Bibliography ... 81

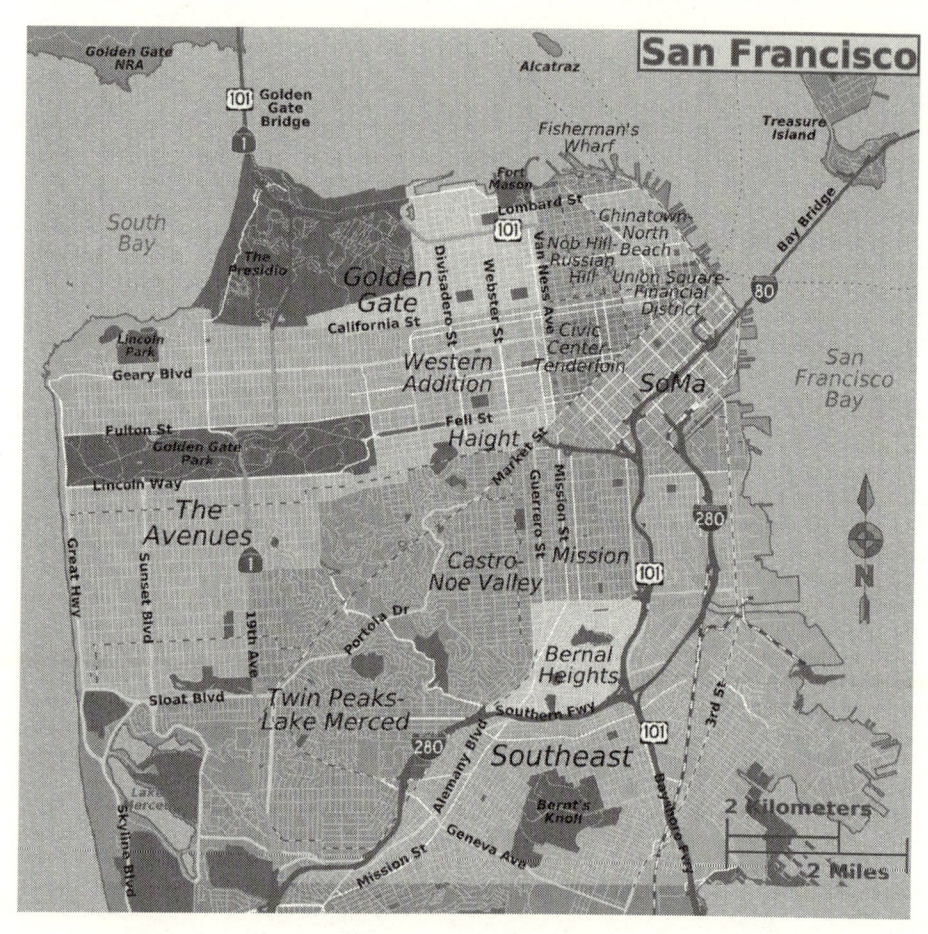

Map 1. San Francisco districts with modern road overlay.

Map 2. The State of California and San Francisco County.

introduction

San Francisco detective Arthur McQuaide was a favorite of Bay-area newspapers during his career. When compared to other lawmen of his era, however, McQuaide seems rather ordinary, by virtue of the press, we are given a glimpse into the crime fighting-life of a man during a critical time in San Francisco's history. The city was just blossoming from its wild and woolly days as a frontier gold rush hub only to be restricted at times by the earthquake of 1906 and the Tong Wars of Chinatown. Still, the city emerged victorious only to become one of the leading commercial, cultural, and industrial centers of the world. This would not have been possible without men like Arthur McQuaide, who, as an enforcer of law and order, have become virtually forgotten in time.

What we know of McQuaide's life is almost entirely taken from the local crime beats of California newspapers. When possible, these reports were corroborated with court and other official records, but many items from pre-earthquake San Francisco are no longer in existence. McQuaide, it seems, was a master of many traits when it came to law enforcement. He dabbled in many aspects of San Francisco crimefighting during his career and it is because of this that we can experience an important and contextual understanding of turn-of-the-century San Francisco.

foreword

By the time he died on New Year's Day, 1939, Arthur T. McQuaide had been a member of the San Francisco Police Department for the better part of a half-century.

The son of working-class Irish immigrants, McQuaide first pinned on a badge in 1898. For the next 40 years, McQuaide would amass an impressive record of arrests while keeping the peace in a city that seemed to be forever in a constant state of change. McQuaide's career would span two centuries, a period in which San Francisco would see tremendous growth while also suffering the deadly calamity of the 1906 earthquake. A crossroads of culture and trade for its entire existence, like other big towns in the American West from Butte, Montana to El Paso, Texas, San Francisco attracted a diverse and colorful cast of characters. Policing such a wild and often rambunctious city was no easy task and McQuaide's career was marked by countless adventures as he made his way up the ranks of one of the frontier's oldest professional law enforcement agencies.

Resurrecting Inspector McQuaide from almost complete obscurity, Erik Wright traces the life of this extraordinary lawman and investigator, introducing us to a rogue's gallery of frontier cops, outlaws on the run, underworld hoodlums, dope dealers and Chinese gangsters. In doing so, Erik has done an impressive bit of detective work himself. Outside of obscure directories, century-old newspapers, and official records, McQuaide's epic life has largely been forgotten.

I first became acquainted with Erik following the release of my first book, "Cowboys and Gangsters: Stories of an Untamed Southwest." Since we've entered each other's orbit, Erik and I have bonded over a mutual affection for the history of the borderlands, the obsessive work that goes into piecing together the long-forgotten stories of lesser-known lawmen and of course the shared trials of writers attempting to stand on the shoulders of the giants that came before us. Historian Marcus Huff has referred to Erik as "the next Leon Metz" and I'd say that Erik more than measures up. With this biography of Inspector McQuaide, Erik adds to his already impressive body of work and there's little doubt that readers can expect more from him in the near future.

A "grass roots historian" in the mode of the late C.L. Sonnichsen, Erik Wright is both a great researcher and a very good man. I am proud to call him my friend. Furthermore, I think the reader will enjoy Erik's tour of the mean streets of the West's premiere metropolis as seen through the eyes of Inspector McQuaide and the men and women of the San Francisco Police Department.

Samuel K. Dolan
Missoula, Montana
May 2018

prologue

After years of bloodshed in San Francisco's Chinatown the local merchants -and police- had seen enough. Brutal assaults and assassinations in the alleyways prompted swift action. On April 26, 1908, Chief of Police William J. Biggy, Captain of Detectives Kelly, and detectives Driscoll, McMahon, and Arthur McQuaide made a "thorough canvass" of Chinatown during which Biggy, a cleanup chief with a shakeup attitude, would no more trust the local agreements or promises made by the Chinese. "The law is to be enforced here," declared Biggy.[1]

Some years before the *San Francisco Chronicle* reported on the violent and vile conditions of Chinatown:

The crack of the pistol last night had a far more ominous sound to the police than the report of a murderer's revolver. It convinced them of the correctness of their suspicions, held for the past week, that another war of the tongs, or Chinese highbinders, has commenced and once started there is no telling where these feuds will end. For several weeks the tongs all over Chinatown have been playing war music in their rooms, and while the shrill, saw-like sound of the Chinese fiddle and the squeak of the Chinese clarinet are common sounds in the Mongolian quarter, those familiar with Chinatown and Chinese ways know that when the music continues until late in the night... some lodge of tongs is at work offering sacrifices to the god of war and preparing to wreak vengeance upon its enemies.[2]

---

[1] *San Francisco Call*, April 27, 1908.
[2] *San Francisco Chronicle*, May 15, 1894.

By 1908 McQuaide was now a veteran detective having inherited the gold rush-era city from his Irish parents. From the 1906 earthquake to the thousands of gambling parlors and the opium dens of Chinatown, McQuaide was beat cop in a city hell bent on destruction.

But it wasn't just Chinatown where vice festered. Places like Morton Street, known as Maiden Lane after the 1906 earthquake, were known as the seedy underbelly of the city. Oscar Lewis described the scene in his book *Bay Window Bohemia*. "It was the hangout, too, of pickpockets, dope peddlers, and thugs of every description… It was scrupulously avoided by the town's respectable women, for to set foot within its confines was considered a serious breach of decorum. To guard against that possibility there was usually a policeman stationed at each end of the street charged with warning away the curious." He continued, "[The alley sheltered] harlots of all nations—including French, Chinese, Negroes, Mexicans, and Americans," and that the street "continued to boom until the entire area was laid waste by the fire of 1906."[3]

McQuaide was not a one-man army, but significantly contributed to the cause of law and order in a city so often plagued by its own growth. With badge and bullets in hand, McQuaide stalked the streets of San Francisco and remained forgotten for nearly a century… until now.

---

[3] Oscar Lewis, *Bay Window Bohemia: An Account of the Brilliant, Artistic World of Gaslit San Francisco*, 1956.

That's my daddy's gun... and the only reason this city's here is because they built it with bullets.

- Kurt Russell as Det. Sgt. Eldon Perry, Jr. in *Dark Blue*

Policing the Underworld

one

A Cauldron of Violence

California boomed after the discovery of gold at Sutter's Mill in 1848 and San Francisco became the central focus for many who sought – and ultimately lost – their fortunes in the west. A city once described as the "Paris of the West", San Francisco saw steady and unparalleled growth as it carved its way towards the twentieth century. In 1864, the newspaper *Alta California* reported that the city was now growing southward and:

A year ago, the waters of the southern bay dashed against a bleak and lonely front, stretching from a rocky barren and forlorn ridge, for half a mile or more. Since then, what a change! The foot of Third Street is now the terminus of the Omnibus Railway, and the hotel whose enterprising proprietor, Farr, has done so much for excavating that thoroughfare to bring cars to the bay waters, is reaping a rich reward for his exertions. Steamboat Point which was but four years ago almost uninhabited waste is now covered with manufactories, shops, saloons and dwellings… on the foot of Third Street the Citizens Gas Company is engaged in an immense enterprise, which when fully carried out must involve an expenditure of one million dollars. This company's land is bounded by Townsend, Second and Berry. They have two lots of 275 feet. In the rear of this front is a precipitous bank of soft rock and dirt, presenting a face towards the bay of 100 feet in height. From this cliff the earth is obtained for filling up the water lots below. At the present, some 75 hands are employed in working into the cliff and carting the rock and dirt to the beach below. Laborers are industriously engaged in 'cribbing' the waterfront lots and filling in the bank… Nature has done much for this enterprise. The precipitous cliff overhanging the bay affords ample materials in way of stone and earth for filling the water lots whilst the shallowness of the waters permits the powerful steam engines to keep otherwise submerged lands dry.[1]

Attracted to this virgin land full of opportunity and perceived wealth were masses of immigrants from around the world. San Francisco was a magnet to single men and entire families from Asia, Australia, South America, Canada, and the British Isles. One such family led by patriarch Patrick McQuaide and his wife, Margaret, arrived in California sometime before 1870. It was then that their son, Arthur, was born on November 9.[2]

A middle child with two elder brothers, Arthur came into the city at a time considered to be one of the most important in the state's history. In 1913, San Francisco businessman Asbury Harpending recalled, "The Silver Age was an intense, booming, hopeful decade . . . Few seem to understand that the decade between 1860 and 1870 was, next to the golden age of the '50s, the most important in the history of California. It was the period of transition from the fierce exploitation of the pioneers who looked only on the region as a thing to be despoiled of its treasures and abandoned. It saw valleys changed into broad oceans of waving grain. It saw the foothills crowned with thrifty vineyards, saw the beginnings of systematic irrigation . . . saw a mighty foreign commerce develop, saw the treasures of the Comstock Lode unlocked, saw a railroad stretch from the Atlantic to the Pacific . . . everyone at last realized

---

[1] *Alta California*, May 2, 1864.
[2] Year:*1880*; Census Place: *San Francisco, California*; Roll: *75*; Family History Film: *1254075*; Page: *545C*; Enumeration District: *108*; Image: *0791*. See also: Arthur McQuaide *Record of Funeral*, January 1, 1939.

that gold was the smallest part of the state's resources and the outlook was as broad as the horizon of mid-ocean."

Still, few details are known about McQuaide's childhood. Like most children of his day, however, McQuaide probably took in the pleasures of street games and fishing at the local pier. One such example, Hobbs Wharf, was a favored spot for locals and in an era of steeped in nostalgia, the *South of Market Journal* wrote, "[*Hobbs Wharf*] was a great place for Sunday and holiday fishing. If one did not get there at an early hour you hadn't a chance to drop your line. There were not many fancy fishing outfits seen then, mostly long bamboo poles. . . There were booths along the wharf where you could rent one and buy your bait. Imagine hundreds of these poles projecting out, about a yard apart. The fish caught were smelt—hundreds of these silvery, graceful fighting fish."[3]

It is entirely unknown whether the young McQuaide felt compelled to follow a career in the police force at this time or what influenced him, but the San Francisco Police Department had long since earned a reputation as a rough and tumble force of officers and detectives charged with fighting some of the most notorious crimes of the frontier west. Yet just 30 years earlier, in his August 1849 inaugural address, John Geary, the first elected alcalde for the city, made the worrisome remark to the freshman city council that the city was, "without a single policeman [*or*] the means of confining a prisoner for an hour."[4]

By August 13 the council had chosen Malachi Fallon as San Francisco's first Chief of Police, then known as a

---

[3] *South of Market Journal*, June 1926.
[4] San Francisco Police Department History, www.sanfranciscopolice.org

marshal. Fallon quickly appointed a deputy captain, three sergeants and 30 officers to comprise the first regular municipal police department in modern San Francisco history.[5]

The initial wave of the city's first officers in 1849 hit the streets with no training, uniforms or equipment of any kind, or even an office from which to conduct police operations. In response to this acute crisis, Fallon housed his men in a school house on Portsmouth Square.

Fallon was born in County Athlone, Ireland in 1814 and moved to New York City with his family when still a boy. As a young man, Fallon ran a saloon frequented by politicians and served for a time as keeper at the Tombs Prison in New York City. But when news of the rich gold strike in California reached the eastern states in late 1848, Fallon ventured west and in July 1849 he was in San Francisco when he wrote, "There were on Trial some persons for Rioting. The merchants of the town having heard of my former connections with Police matters, called to see me and offered inducements to remain and organize a police [*force*]. The council met and appointed me Chief of Police at a salary of six thousand dollars a year, to have the whole control of appointments and [*assistant*] three sergeants and 30 men."[6]

The move by city leaders to appoint a relative novice like Fallon was virtually unheard of. But in a city plagued by drunken and violent gold seekers including the vicious Sydney Ducks gang, anything was possible.

---

[5] Ibid.
[6] Ibid.

Known first as the Sydney Coves Gang, the "Ducks" were a ruthless group of bandits from Australia who made easy pickings on the booming waterfront city. It wasn't until December 1848 that news of the gold rush reached Australian shores. However, by May of 1851, an estimated 11,000 Australians had set their sails towards America with an estimated 7,500 of those coming directly from Sydney. Historian Richard Hough further analyzed the contemporary scene and, with San Francisco's population at 36,000 in 1852, the proportion of Aussie gold seekers and ex-convicts flooding the Bay area was astronomical. Hough further explained that the Australians were viewed by the Americans with "extreme suspicion" and that "the crimes of a few brought down prejudice upon the whole."

Still, those Australians in early San Francisco sought to cause wide ranging mayhem. Some of the Ducks had apparently learned their craft in the Australian bush when aboriginal hunters set fire to hollow trees to flush out the game inside. The Ducks took this tactic to full effect in San Francisco by lighting homes and commercial buildings ablaze to force the occupants outside who inevitably where holding their most valuable items. In response to the immigrant violence, vigilance committees were formed and arrested at least 91 suspected Ducks gang members. Four of these Aussie hooligans were subsequently hanged in front of a mob of thousands of onlookers while others were deported and some simply disappeared.[7]

Vigilante justice in early gold rush California was not always at the hands of organized committees. In 1854, a group of three men led by Mexican War Veteran Captain

---

[7] Robert Hughes. *The Fatal Shore: The Epic of Australia's Founding*, 1987.

Johnathan Davis were trekking down an established trail in Rocky Canyon in El Dorado County just south of Lake Tahoe. In the same area six Chinese had been killed and the three travelers did not know that the same bandits lay in wait for their next victims along the trail.

11 men of Australian, British, American, French, and Mexican descent met their fate soon after they ambushed the party. Davis' fellow travelers were killed or mortally wounded, but Davis, a calm and deadly shot finished off seven of the outlaws with his brace of Colt revolvers before gutting one man and slicing the nose off the other. After the violent and deadly affair regional newspapers began to doubt Davis' account, but frustrated by the media's spin, Davis offered to take any reporter to the scene of the crime and view the graves of the fallen highwaymen.

Nobody accepted the offer.[8]

By 1856, citizens in San Francisco voted in favor of a charter that would govern the city for the remainder of the century. The charter dictated, the police department was to be governed by a commission made up of the mayor, the police court judge and the chief executive officer of the department, now re-designated from city marshal to chief of police. The police chief, like that of mayor and police court judge, were to be elected seats, but at two-year intervals while the city's police officers were to be removed only for cause.[9]

---

[8] John Boessenecker. *Gold Dust & Gunsmoke: Tales of Gold Rush Outlaws, Gunfighters, Lawmen, and Vigilantes*, 1999.
[9] San Francisco Police Department History, www.sanfranciscopolice.org

By the time McQuaide was born in 1870 the city had successfully dowsed its first reign of significant violence. But, with the recent ending of the Civil War a massive population swell occurred which saw San Francisco County's population explode from 56,802 in 1860 to a staggering 149,473 in 1870. By the next decade the population had again grown to 233,959 residents. The city was rapidly becoming the destination on America's west coast which had been made even easier with the completion of the Transcontinental Railroad in May of 1869. These factors opened the city up to a host of economic, social, cultural, and often nefarious opportunities that would allow young men like Arthur McQuaide to fully embrace the right – or wrong – side of law and order.[10]

---

[10] www.bayareacensus.ca.gov, *Population by County, 1860-2000*.

two
California or Bust

Arthur's father, Patrick, was a green-blooded Irishman. It remains unclear what brought him to America, but while living in San Francisco as an older man he noted on a voter registration that he was naturalized in Lowell, Massachusetts on October 28, 1852 when he was only 21 years old. It was there that he arrived with his parents, Charles and Mary as well as his numerous siblings.[1]

There were dozens of young men named Patrick McQuaide entering the country at that time so fleshing out which one was the father of the future San Francisco Police detective is virtually impossible. Still, young Patrick was one of the tens of thousands of Irish men and women who sought refuge in America during the Great Famine.

In 1844 the population of Ireland had grown to a staggering 8.4 million people. Many of these individuals had lives centered upon the production of potatoes, but in 1845, the Phytophthora infestans, the potato blight, had arrived and began to decimate the country's principal crop. By 1851 decision makers in London opted that providing aide to the struggling Irish population would only create dependency and, in the wake of 1.1 million deaths from the famine, an additional 1.5 million sailed to America.

---

[1] Year: *1850*; Census Place: *Lowell, Middlesex, Massachusetts*; Roll: *M432_327*; Page: *288B*; Image: *191*

The Great Famine came on the heels of a country in absolute economic and social destitution. In the 1830s, the Frenchman Gustave de Beaumont traveled through Ireland and wrote, "the Indian in his forest and the Negro in chains… in all countries… paupers may be discovered, but an entire nation of paupers is what was never seen until it was shown in Ireland."

During this time a majority of the Irish population lived on small farms scratched from the earth in minute, windowless huts. Children married each other at young ages with virtually no hope for the future. When the blight struck the country many people quickly succumbed to fevers by eating infected potatoes while some in London called upon the blight to rid the British Isles of an unwanted and burdensome population. British civil servant and colonial administrator Charles Edward Trevelyan believed the famine was a sign of God's wrath upon the Irish and was ultimately a "mechanism for removing surplus population."

Desperate to escape the deadly conditions in Ireland a mass exodus occurred. Philanthropist Steven de Vere traveled as a steerage passenger aboard a ship bound for Canada in 1847 and penned his troublesome observations. "Hundreds of poor people, men, women and children of all ages, from the driveling idiot of ninety to the babe just born, huddled together without air, wallowing in filth and breathing a fetid atmosphere, sick in body, dispirited in heart… dying without voice of spiritual consolation, and buried in the deep without the rites of the church."[2]

---

[2] Constitutional Rights Foundation, *Bill of Rights in Action*, vol. 26, no. 2, "Population Perils"

Upon their arrival to America, however, the Irish still faced a difficult existence. Historian William Shannon observed the irony of the Irish immigrant in America. "The history of the Irish in America is founded on a paradox. The Irish were a rural people in Ireland and became a city people in the United States... Beneath these circumstances, there lay a still more profound motivation. The Irish rejected the land for the land had rejected them... [The Irish] turned away from the fields of Ireland with a sense of relief... American cities were in their infancy when the Irish came. Their rise and the rise of the Irish in American life when hand in hand. In Ireland, the Irish had inherited history and suffered it. In America, they became the makers of history."[3]

Yet as soon as the Irish arrived anti-Irish sentiment began. Fueled by the vitriol from London, cruel political cartoons depicting the beleaguered Irish as drunk, brutish, and lazy. Throughout the country signs depicting a common message of "No Irish Need Apply" further hampered their individual economic prospects. With the outbreak of the Civil War, however, the Irish were given an opportunity to redeem their standing in the public eye. Many of the new Irish arrivals fought bravely and fiercely in a war for which they felt resentful of. The 1863 Draft Riots in New York City best illustrate this feeling as many of the Irish could not understand the need to fight in a war to free slaves when it was the freedmen who were regarded as competition to the few jobs made available to most of able-bodied Irish men.

Frustrated with the restrictive opportunities in the east waves of Irish men, women, and family units took to the

---

[3] From: The Other Immigrants: Comparing the Irish in Australia and the United States by Malcolm Campbell. *Journal of American Ethnic History*, vol. 14, no. 3.

western trails. With strong backs and a fighting spirit the Irish made up one-third of the immigrant population in the western frontier. Their contributions to the construction of railroads and work in the mines also helped to give rise to the popular perception of the Irish in the west as gambler and gunfighter. Patrick McQuaide's movements between the time he was naturalized in Massachusetts and his arrival in California are entirely unknown. Throughout his life, however, he was noted as a "laborer" so the possibility exists that McQuaide, whether in California or another western territory, worked as a miner or road builder. In his 1883 trial for the murder of Irish gunman James Leavy, fellow Irishman Johnny Murphy, a prospector and professional gambler spoke to the presiding judge. "Your honor, I thank you and the jury, but I desire to say that I have lived all my life on the frontier. I was honorably discharged from the navy, when a young man, on the coast of Florida, and came right through to the frontier. I have been amongst rough men all my life, have stopped many a bad fight, and never before been in any trouble..."[4]

Murphy's statement could likely be applied to many Irish men in the west. The clear majority are lost to time, but their individual contributions to the establishment of this country in the decades before and after the Civil War cannot be overlooked. What remains clear, however, is that Patrick McQuaide lived a life typical of so many of his countrymen and sought a better future for himself and, in the end, for his family, in San Francisco.

Patrick McQuaide married Margaret Gleeson on September 9, 1856 in Lowell. Margaret, another Irish native, had four

---

[4] Erik Wright, *Gamblers, Guns & Gavels: Collected Works on Arizona Gambling Violence* (Tripaw Press, 2015).

children with Patrick including Arthur.[5] By the time Arthur was born the family was living on Gilbert Street in San Francisco's South of Market District. A large neighborhood south of the center of the city's action, young Arthur probably still did experience or was at the very least aware of the vices of San Francisco. In 1876, the city's so-called Barbary Coast, a red-light district named for the north African coast favored by pirates and slave traders, was described:

The Barbary Coast is the haunt of the low and the vile of every kind. The petty thief, the house burglar, the tramp, the whoremonger, lewd women, cutthroats, murderers, all are found here. Dance-halls and concert-saloons, where blear-eyed men and faded women drink vile liquor, smoke offensive tobacco, engage in vulgar conduct, sing obscene songs and say and do everything to heap upon themselves more degradation, are numerous. Low gambling houses, thronged with riot-loving rowdies, in all stages of intoxication, are there. Opium dens, where heathen Chinese and God-forsaken men and women are sprawled in miscellaneous confusion, disgustingly drowsy or completely overcome, are there. Licentiousness, debauchery, pollution, loathsome disease, insanity from dissipation, misery, poverty, wealth, profanity, blasphemy, and death, are there. And Hell, yawning to receive the putrid mass, is there also.[6]

It would not be long before Arthur, a bright young man with a mind for mathematics, would be summoned, perhaps unexpectedly, into the world of crime fighting.

---

[5] *Massachusetts, Town and Vital Records, 1620-1988*
[6] Benjamin Estelle Lloyd, *Lights and Shades of San Francisco* (1876).

three
Rookie

By the time Arthur McQuaide reached adulthood he had a recognized ability by his peers as an intelligent young man. In December of 1892, McQuaide, still a relative stranger to the print media of San Francisco, made his first appearance in *The Morning Call*.

The event which was reported upon was also the likely catalyst for McQuaide's intentional -or unintentional- entry into public service with the police department. *The Morning Call* reported that on Friday, December 2, attorney Andrew J. Clunie and auditor and elections commissioner Smiley went at it with fists during a heated meeting over elections tampering. "A Free Fight, in Which There Were a Good Many Participants, but Few Injuries" read the sub-headline. To help settle matters during the aggressive meeting "a man named McQuaide" was brought forward "who is supposed to know something about the alterations of tally-sheets…"

Despite McQuaide's apparent willingness to lend his expertise to the matter both men at the center of the fight refused to listen to reason. Death threats and mocking insults were thrown back and forth until the men were nearly ejected from the room by force. "Lunch did nothing to cool the matter… [and] Smiley's bodyguard was the center of attraction, and when he got free he had an eye about swollen shut, and he was last seen making for a butcher-shop for a piece of raw meat to cure his disfiguration…"

The same issue reported on current conditions of the city and foreshadowed the gritty, wretched underworld that McQuaide was now embarking into. "There were nineteen deaths in this city during the month of November… There was almost a continuous downpour all day yesterday in this city, and last evening the rain was coming down in torrents. The bank along the south shore became soaked and huge slices of earth succumbed to the erosive actions of the waves."[1]

Despite McQuaide's efforts in the elections commission brawl he does not seem to have been appointed an official officer with the department until August 11, 1898 at age 27. He was issued badge number 1150 and is believed to have lived in the same area around Gilbert Street in the South of Market district where he grew up.[2]

A neighborhood once described as San Francisco's Skid Row, the "SoMa" district had long been a refuge for the motley society known to populate the city. In the 1860's the district became attractive to single men and prompted a so-called "hotel tradition" in the area. This tradition dates to the gold rush when single miners and prospectors would pass the winter "pursuing sinful amusements of the city, joining sailors on leave and agricultural laborers in the valleys." In 1871, the year McQuaide was born, newspaper editor Henry George described what he saw in the district. He observed that migrant workers "disappeared" after the

---

[1] *The Morning Call*, December 3, 1892.
[2] Personal correspondence with John Boessenecker, August 10, 2016.

wheat harvest "into the flophouses of San Francisco-to come back next season like so many ragged cows."

The next year another observed wrote of the "tramps" he met in the area as well as a growing population of runaway sailors, reformed street thieves, bankrupt German painters, and old soldiers.

But by the time that McQuaide could become fully aware of his surroundings in the district conditions had not improved. Labor agitation of the period drove migrant farm workers out of the urban spaces and into the fertile valleys of central California. This, in turn, drove masses of Chinese workers out of the rural areas and back into the cities. Furthermore, the South of Market district held one-third of the city's pawnshops by 1900. A charitable woodyard in the district operated by The Associated Charities allowed "penniless men to chop wood at ten cents an hour in exchange for a meal, lodging, or a ferry boat ride across the bay."[3]

Yet San Francisco's woes were not just for those in the South of Market district. In 1882, just after Virgil Earp of Tombstone had been maimed in an unsuccessful assassination attempt, the troubles of the so-called Tombstone Gamblers' War spilled out into the streets of San Francisco. Historian Peter Brand uncovered the story of the vicious feud between the Earps and those established Irishmen in the city who fought to maintain control of their gambling interests. When Virgil Earp arrived he quickly established his own gambling den on Morton Street (now known as Maiden Lane) just south of Chinatown. The

---

[3] Alvin Averbach, "San Francisco's South of Market District, 1850-1890: The Emergence of a Skid Row". *California Historical Quarterly*, vol. 52, no. 3.

second-floor faro room, described as the Tiger's Lair, was complete with a police alarm, thickly-padded stairway, a door without a knob, and cut in the door to watch over those ascending the stairway. Dublin Lyons, another old Tombstone gambler, had established his own gambling parlor nearby and, fueled by past animosity towards the Earp brothers, sought revenge. *The Oakland Tribune* reported, "[Lyons'] hatred toward the Earps was such that even at the risk of hurting his own game, he took steps to have their gambling house closed up when they opened on Morton Street, and many a raid on their place was credited to Dublin."

Brand further explained that with some heavy political influence and a little Irish muscle, Lyons was successful in his quest to wipe the Earps out of the San Francisco gambling scene. The *San Francisco Chronicle* reported on police raids on nine gambling establishments including Earp's on August 1, 1882. "At 15 Morton Street, the posse under Sergeant Bethel broke in the door and ascended to the second story, where the gambling rooms are located, and succeeded in arresting fifteen persons and in capturing the entire layout of checks, boxes, cards, etc., and $1,422 in cash. The game at this place was conducted by Virgil Earp, a member of the notorious Earp family of Arizona who carried his arm in a sling from the result of some recent fracas."[4]

What McQuaide saw and experienced in his formative years in the South of Market district likely had a lasting influence on the young man. McQuaide left no letters,

---

[4] Peter Brand, "The Killing of Charlie Storms by Luke Short: Being A Closer at the Gunfight and Its Consequences" Wild West History Association *Journal*, August 2015.

diaries, or family reminiscences, but his actions with the police department as reported by a variety of regional news publications of the time speak for him. Despite the apparent ominous and sinister feel of the McQuaide's early San Francisco, a city defined by gambling dens and violent street thugs, the police would encounter their share of comical, but often dangerous individuals. In the summer of 1899 an escaped mental patient named Edgar Garnett, previously accused of harassing "women of society" with written letters, escaped from the Stockton Insane Asylum. During his break for freedom, Garnett took refuge in his parent's home at 35 Essex Street and threatened to kill himself with a razor, but due to the poor health of Garnett's mother, police opted not to force entry into the house.

With no recourse left the police set up surveillance on the home day and night. Officers were given clear instructions that if Garnett left the home he was to be followed and arrested, but little movement was seen at the house for many hours. With daybreak came information from the suspect's father who told police that his son had expressed his intentions of walking to a local library. Summoned to Essex Street was Arthur McQuaide, who, "had only a few minutes on the lookout when Edgar came out of the house. McQuaide quietly followed him till he reached Second and Mission streets, where he entered a store to purchase a morning paper."[5]

McQuaide followed Garnett and "in an instant had the handcuffs over Garnett's wrists," the *Call* reported. During the arrest Garnett tried to reach into his vest pocket, but McQuaide acted quickly and pulled a razor out of the suspect's pocket. "Then Garnett became indignant and

---

[5] *San Francisco Call*, July 24, 1899.

demanded the reason of such 'outrageous treatment'..." McQuaide told the suspect that he was Edgar Garnett who had recently escaped from the Stockton Asylum, but the man defiantly argued that his name was Smith and he came in from mining in Plumas County.

McQuaide took his chances and rang for the patrol wagon to arrive. Garnett continued with his challenging attitude and threatened to starve himself to death while in custody, but a moment later asked for a meal. Police believed that Garnett was looking for a knife for which to kill himself.

The *Call* also reported that Garnett, a graduate of Harvard University, was the son of a well-known assayer. It added that his uncle, Major Robert Seldon Garnett came to the area in 1849 and was the designer of the Seal of California. "The young man's hallucination is that he is irresistible to women, married or single, and he pesters them with his attentions."[6]

All was not fun and games for a year later in the summer of 1900, two of McQuaide's fellow police officers were badly beaten during their duty. "Police officers John Gallaway and Henry Heinz entered the Receiving Hospital last night dripping with blood..." reported the *San Francisco Call*. The paper added that the assaulted officers had been on a plain-clothes detail to arrest "vagrants and beggars" but during their undercover work the two officers eyed a large crowd around the front of the Orlando House near Sixth and Howard streets. The boarding house was trying to rid itself of unwanted guests and in attempting to enforce the law and the wishes of the house landlord, the men were viciously assaulted by a boarder named Moss. Both officers

---

[6] Ibid.

were knocked down by the hulking Moss and the situation was made more troublesome when nearby vagrants came to the aide of Moss and began to kick and punch the downed officers. One of the policemen eventually cracked Moss over the head with his revolver and took refuge inside a nearby grocery store. "Officer McQuaide arrived opportunely on the scene and by a liberal use of his stick quelled further trouble."[7]

With the dawn of the twentieth century now casting on the horizon, McQuaide was quickly earning a reputation for himself as a local beat cop who, through force and quick mindedness, would bring help stability to the violent streets of San Francisco.

---

[7] *San Francisco Call*, June 6, 1900.

Portsmouth Square, San Francisco circa 1851.

THE FENIAN GUY FAWKES.

Anti-Irish propaganda in the mid to late nineteenth century portrayed struggling Irish immigrants as lazy, violent, and drunk.

During the raid growth of San Francisco in the first few years following the discovery of gold in California crime swept the city and the region. The lynching of James P. Casey and Charles Cora by the San Francisco Committee of Vigilance in 1856.

Stockton Street looking north towards Angel Island, circa 1870.

In James Mahony's 1847 illustration Scene at Skibbereen, West Cork, *published in the* Illustrated London News, *the plight of the Irish farmer was seen during the potato famine.*

Chinese farm workers, California, circa 1900.

Ross Alley, San Francisco Chinatown, circa 1900.

four

Big Trouble in Little China

In the fall of 1900 McQuaide was attached to a special detail of the San Francisco Police Department charged with eradicating the corrupting elements of the city's Chinese district. Known as Chinatown Squads, these details were small, aggressive units often characterized by a "take no prisoner" attitude. Many contemporary photos of the Chinatown Squads throughout the early 1900s show detectives in plain street clothes brandishing sledgehammers and axes; tools used to break the back of vice and violence in Chinatown. These photos also typically featured illegal contraband seized by police such as the weapons of street warfare used by the Chinese enforcers such as swords, hatchets, and other brutal and exotic weapons.

The department held firm a policy of cycling the squads out on a routine basis. This was in part to help keep the faces of those enforcing law and order fresh to the Chinese criminals and secondly to help discourage corruption within their own ranks. On November 8, 1900, McQuaide would get his chance in policing the violent Chinese district.

A Sergeant McManus, it was reported, along with his team of officers were to be replaced after only three months of service to the department in Chinatown. "Their record for arrests and the amount of fines collected has not been exceeded by any previous squad during a similar period. The total number of arrests was 854 and the total numbers of fines collected was $6,036.50. They were detailed for duty in the Chinese quarter at a critical time and by their actions have shown that the confidence reposed in them by Chief Sullivan was not misplaced."[1]

In addition to the number of arrests and total fines collected it was reported that the squad served 137 search warrants, caught 15 lottery drawings, and closed 13 lottery agencies "patronized by whites."

Replacing the squad was Arthur McQuaide along with his sergeant, a man named Brophy, and five other officers. "Most of them have seen service in Chinatown before and are all experienced officers."[2]

The Chinatown squads came on the heels of the most violent period for the San Francisco Chinese. From roughly 1870 to 1890 there was an intense period of anti-Chinese sentiment and violence throughout the country. This anti-Chinese agitation drove established Chinese populations and family units from many rural farming and mining settlements in California to the urban chaos of San Francisco. Masses of discharged white laborers began to persecute the Chinese, who were taking filling out local jobs throughout the city for cheaper pay. This anti-Chinese feeling culminated on July 24, 1877 when several hundred men rampaged San Francisco and attacked any Chinese in sight.

Reacting to this "long depression" the San Francisco Riot began in earnest. "Everything was orderly until an anti-Coolie [Asian laborer] procession pushed its way into the audience and insisted that the speakers say something about

---

[1] *San Francisco Call*, November 8, 1900.
[2] Ibid.

the Chinese," wrote historian Selig Perlman. "This was refused and thereupon the crowd which had gathered on the outskirts of the meeting attacked a passing Chinaman and started the cry, 'On to Chinatown.'"[3]

The vengeful mob set their sights on Chinese laundromats across the city, but the rioting was just beginning. With the police force overwhelmed, citizens on both sides of the cultural equation began warring. The *San Francisco Chronicle* reported, "The band then moved in groups down Howard Street to Second under the lead of a drunken man of gigantic stature, who rend the air with his demoniacal yells... Every Chinese house had evidently been carefully listed beforehand, for on the whole line of march and on either side of the streets there was not left a single one which was not utterly and completely sacked."

Reacting to the outpouring of violence, the *New York Times* reported later that, "With characteristic cowardice the San Francisco mob threatened Chinese residents, and has wrecked several Chinese shops and houses... People who sack Chinese houses and stone Chinamen are not workingmen. San Francisco calls them 'hoodlums,' a term which includes everything that is base and mean. The hoodlum is a non-producer, loafer and bully. The hoodlum class think this is a good time to signify their hatred of law and order."[4]

The Chinese Exclusion Act of 1882, signed by President Chester A. Arthur, halted Chinese immigration for ten

---

[3] *History of Labour in the United States: Nationalisation (1860-1877)* by J. B. Andrews. *Upheaval and Reorganisation (since 1876)* by Selig Perlman, 1921. MacMillan Company.

[4] *New York Times*, July 26, 1877.

years. But, the 1906 earthquake would help those already in the country, many illegally, become citizens after countless official records were destroyed by fire and the Chinese population signed "paper certificates" attesting to their natural citizenship.

Still, the law and order element mentality of the city's leaders persisted for decades. Reacting as a maligned population with little recourse for income and social standing in the greater community, many Chinese opted for illegal gambling and opium dens as well as more sinister crimes like racketeering, prostitution, and murder.

It was in this latter climate of social disorder that Brophy's squad was disbanded and the officers redistributed in March 1901. Little record of their service remains and McQuaide would be transferred again to that of a regular detective.[5]

---

[5] *San Francisco Call*, March 5, 1901. For more on the Chinatown squads and crime in San Francisco's Chinese quarter consult Richard H. Dillon, *Hatchet Men: The Story of the Tong Wars in San Francisco's Chinatown* (1962).

five
Lost Years

By mid-1901, McQuaide was back to doing what he did best: tracking down and cuffing bunco men, robbers, and violent street thugs. McQuaide was to become the bane of the San Francisco urban outlaw.

The police force in San Francisco at the time was markedly different from decades past. The city knew it was growing and often looked to the New York Police Department as an example. As part of the overall progressive movement taking hold in America the department opted for a dramatic reorganization. The rank of lieutenant was added throughout the force to establish another level of supervisory responsibility and the department was transferred to local city control by 1900. Reacting to this new era in the department the city constructed an elaborate, multi-story Hall of Justice on Portsmouth Square. By 1906, however, the building was destroyed from ground shaking and fire and one witness described it as the "damnest [sic] finest ruins" in the city.

Nonetheless, the police – and the criminals – persisted.

From the late summer of 1901 until the end of 1904, McQuaide was named in several newspapers beat reports of local crime busting. McQuaide and his fellow detectives were maintaining their reputations as "bunco busters" and men who would often resort to physical violence to nab their suspects.

However, little evidence remains of the immediate years that follow. In the summer of 1903, however, McQuaide's older brother, Daniel, a teamster, died tragically in San Francisco.

On August 20, Daniel was rushed to the Central Emergency Hospital after a truck had run him over and broken his spine. He died that day and was buried at the Holy Cross Catholic Cemetery in Colma, California.[1]

Beat cops and detectives like McQuaide, who had worked tirelessly to extinguish vice from their city, would soon be faced with a new and insurmountable challenge. Their task would be one entirely unrivaled in the annals of California history before or since and while McQuaide's role remains unclear, he likely exhibited the same bravery and leadership qualities during the Great San Francisco Earthquake of 1906 as he did while on routine patrol in years past.

---

[1] California, County Birth, Marriage, and Death Records, 1830-1980. California Department of Public Health. City of San Francisco Mortuary Records, 1901-1905, Book R, pp. 25-26.

six

The Horrible Dream of 1906

At 5:12 a.m. on April 18, 1906, a violent foreshock woke many from their sleep in the San Francisco area. About 25 seconds later those who weren't disturbed by the earth's rumblings were thrown from their beds by one of the most devastating and violent earthquakes in history. The shocks punctuated the lasted some 45 to 60 seconds and the earthquake was felt from southern Oregon to south of Los Angeles and inland as far as central Nevada. Estimates of the earthquake's strength range from a high XII to a IX on the Modified Mercalli Intensities scale.

Eyewitness Arthur C. Poore recalled the devastation:

> At the corners of Larkin and Polk, on Golden Gate Avenue we found a perfect hell of fire. It was now feeding on a solidly built section of wooden buildings; I shall never forget the fierceness and viciousness of those flames roaring like a blast furnace, and their steady crackle like musketry fire…
>
> The upward draft of such a fire was terrific, the air rushing in from all sides to a common center and being sucked upward. It was estimated that the smoke rose to a height of a thousand feet. To show the tremendous power of the draft, great pieces of sheet iron roofing ten feet square were torn loose after being nearly burned free from the wooden roof

and whirled upward into the air, out of sight like leaves in an autumn gale. I watched a three-story dwelling house catch from the next house and timed it with my watch. In twenty minutes the cellar remained, nothing more. Not even charred and blackened timbers. Combustion was complete and absolute…[1]

In the wake of the devastation an estimated 3,000 people were killed, many of whom were fatalities by the ensuing fires. Half of the city's 400,000 residents were left homeless and looting was rampant as the survivors took refuge in tent cities. Reacting to the threat of additional looting, San Francisco mayor Eugene Schmitz took drastic measures with his executive order. "The Federal Troops, the members of the Regular Police Force and all Special Police Officers have been authorized by me to kill any and all persons found engaged in Looting or in the Commission of Any Other Crime."

Three days after the earthquake, *General Order No. 12* divided the city into six military districts and stated that all law enforcement divisions were to conduct themselves in "temperate action in dealing with the unfortunate people who are suffering from the awful catastrophe that has befallen them."

The warning came on the heels of citizen reports of military misconduct. Bay-area citizens had complained of unnecessary evacuations and, more dire, implementation of Schmitz's order to shoot and kill looters, or even presumed looters. The reports of citizens shot because of the Mayor's

---

[1] *The Argonaut*, Spring 1990.

Proclamation vary greatly and range from one dozen up to one hundred citizens.[2]

The Mayor reacted later to further and likely greater threats to his city. The fires that swept the city in the immediate aftermath of the earthquake were a real concern for authorities attempting to restore order and the Mayor knew action was needed. On April 22 he issued the following order:

> Lights are permitted in houses between Sunset and 10 p.m. only, unless sentinels are convinced that some latitude should be allowed in case of sickness.
>
> As all chimneys were more or less injured by the earthquake, no fires will be permitted in houses in grates, stoves or fireplaces unless the occupants hold a certificate issued by an authorized chimney inspector. Said certificate to be posted in a conspicuous place in front of the building.
>
> The importance of this provision is emphasized by the fact that no effective means are at hand for stopping fires.
>
> Our greatest danger in the immediate future may be expected from unavoidable unsanitary conditions and every person is cautioned that to violate in the slightest degree the instructions from the officers will be a crime that cannot be adequately punished.

---

[2] https://www.nps.gov/prsf/learn/historyculture/1906-earthquake-law-enforcement.htm

> All persons, except suspicious characters, will be permitted to pass sentinels without interruption.[3]

In the aftermath of the earthquake many of the city's police officers were charged with the task of rebuilding the city. Ranked officers often oversaw cleanup and construction crews while troops from the Presidio helped to enforce law and order. The two groups also worked together in distributing food to the mass of evacuees. In 1910, Captain Thomas Duke penned a narrative of the department's involvement in the disaster and recovery. "As the shock shattered the principal water mains, the fire department was practically helpless and as a result, the fires which were started by the overturning of stoves, crossing of electric wires, the liberation of chemicals by breakage of containers, etc., rapidly spread until a territory of 4.7 square miles in the heart of the city was burned, and a loss approximately estimated at $275,000,000 was incurred," Duke wrote. "As the earthquake rendered the jails unsafe, he ordered that all petty offenders be released, while those charged with more serious offenses were sent to San Quentin State Prison."[4]

Duke observed that the common criminal found easy pickings in the wake of the city's destruction. Reports reached headquarters that thieves were burglarizing wrecked stores and deserted homes, and it was also learned that in the Mission district the body of a woman was found, the finger upon which she wore several valuable rings having been amputated, evidently by some thief.

---

[3] Thomas S. Duke, *Synopsis of the San Francisco Police and Municipal Records of the Greatest Catastrophe in American History*. 1910.
[4] Ibid.

The next report was to the effect that rowdies were breaking into saloons and helping themselves to liquor… As the police were busy conveying the wounded to the temporary hospitals and had no time to arrest thieves even if caught in the act, and no place to incarcerate them if arrested…"

After the mayor's order to have looters killed was issued, Brigadier General Frederick Funston arrived with troops at the ready and quickly found a looter in the process of robbing a jewelry store at the corner of Post and Grant avenues. A soldier under Funston shot and killed the looter and reports indicate the soldier left the looter's body to smolder in the fire as he moved on in his patrol.

As more and more bodies began to fill the city's morgue, a facility designed for light use, the city's Central Police Station became a temporary holding facility for the dozens of corpses being brought in. However, as fire and crumbling walls threatened the station the bodies were temporarily buried in nearby Portsmouth Square.

"On the morning of the earthquake it became apparent that immediate steps must be taken to prevent a famine. Police officers were therefore detailed to seize all suitable conveyances and remove the contents of all grocery stores which were in danger of being burned. This work was kept up for three days and nights, and as a result the contents of 390 grocery stores were delivered to the refugees."[5]

On April 19, a squad of nine officers with the department boarded sea-going vessels loaded with provisions which

---

[5] Ibid.

were already anchored in port. The path to the Pacific was blocked to disallow the ships from leaving until more supplies could be brought in by rail.

Duke noted that the tenacity of the officers of the city helped to preserve many of the official police records.

> When it became apparent that the Hall of Justice would be destroyed by fire, all valuable police records were removed to Portsmouth Square and left in charge of a detail of officers, consisting of Detectives Charles Taylor, George McMahon and others. These officers were provided with provisions, but no water was obtainable. The fire rapidly surrounded the square and the officers became prisoners. The heat was terrific and the cinders, which were falling like hail, were constantly igniting the canvas spread over the records. As there was a saloon across the street which had not at that time caught fire, a raid was made on the place, and for the next twenty-four hours bottled beer was used to keep the canvas from igniting, and thus the records were saved.

He concluded that had it not been for the bravery of the city's firemen and police officers, San Francisco would have been virtually uninhabitable. "A volume would be required to record the many heroic deeds performed by the firemen and police during those three eventful days and nights. And it must he remembered that most them labored with little nourishment and no sleep, and with the knowledge that their homes were destroyed and the fate of their families unknown," Duke wrote.

Once safely back home in Massachusetts, Arthur Poore, who saw firsthand the destructive forces of the fire caused by the earthquake, recalled the trauma. "As I look back on it all now, it seems as though we conducted ourselves with a matter-of-fact demeanor, as if our lives were moving in the usual way. The strangeness of it all, the unheard-of conditions in which I was moving never came home to me until long after when I was safely back in Boston. Then I would get to thinking of those events at night and lie awake until two o'clock in the morning, wondering if it had only been a strange and horrible dream."[6]

---

[6] *The Argonaut*, Spring 1990.

Jesse B. Cook's Chinatown Squad, 1905. Cook would later serve as the city's Chief of Police following the 1906 earthquake. Note the axes and mauls used to break down doors during the squad's raids throughout Chinatown.

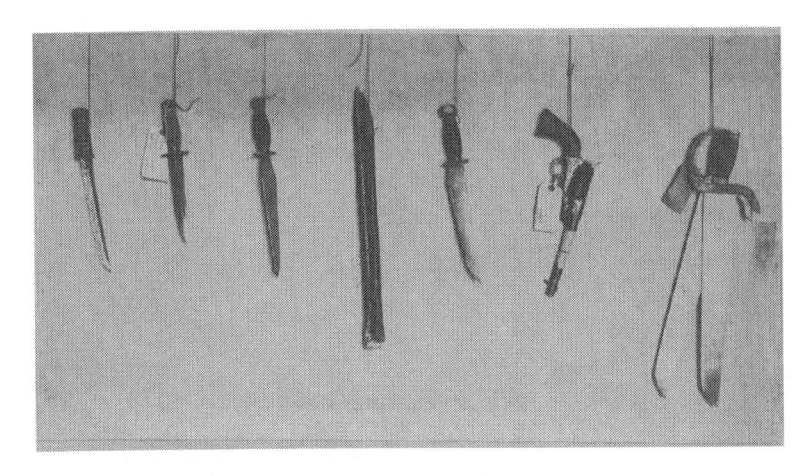

Confiscated Highbinder weapons from San Francisco Chinatown.

Digital Collection, Bancroft Library, University of California at Berkley

San Francisco Chinatown alley, circa 1900-1920.

Mission District in flames after the 1906 earthquake.

Federal troops helped to guard the city's destroyed Hall of Justice after the 1906 earthquake.

A last message is sent by wire in front of the ruined Hall of Justice just before the advancing flames took over the area.

James Trammell, a man wanted in Arkansas for a 1909 murder, was captured by McQuaide and his partner Thomas Murphy in 1911 while Trammell was living under an alias.

seven

Arkansas Fugitive

In the years that followed the Great Earthquake of 1906 the city and its municipal departments quickly rebounded.

The department constructed a new Hall of Justice with a reinforced steel frame in 1912 as well as district headquarters at Richmond, Park, and Ingleside which were all opened in 1910. These were followed by stations built at Potrero, Harbor, and Northern districts in 1913. In addition to building on the department's infrastructure the city leaders looked to innovate the department as well. In 1908 chief Jesse Cook appointed three dedicated motorcycle officers in what would evolve to be the first motorcycle detail in the country and the department was also one of the first to use fingerprinting as a form of criminal identification. In 1913, chief David White hired three female protective officers to join the ranks of the police department.

While the city's Board of Supervisors budgeted only $3,600 for three positions, 22 women looked to apply. "Two and twenty women ready to gird their waists, if necessary, with a belt and revolver, and to pin on their intrepid, kindly, ambitious bosoms the insignia of the peace officer, are waiting the decision of the board of supervisors. In the matter of the appointment policewomen," reported the *San Francisco Call*. "Los Angeles invented the idea of the police woman and the fashion has circulated back and forth throughout the country. Chicago has just named 10... What the duty of these officers in petticoats shall be, whether they will be required to wear uniforms of blue and brass buttons, to be bedecked with a star, to carry a revolver and a club, has not yet been decreed."[1]

It was in this era of urban and social renewal that Arthur McQuaide would make one of the most significant arrests of his policing career. Along with his partner, fellow detective Thomas Murphy, McQuaide locked their cuffs on a wanted murderer from Arkansas who had been conspicuously living among the San Francisco working class for at least a year. But, through solid detective work and a tip from the man's purported wife, the detectives had their man.

In his later years, James Henry Trammell never spoke of what happened in Paragould, a small city in northeast Arkansas, over a half century before. In a letter, likely written by a sister to Trammell's daughter Zula in New South Wales, Australia, it explains, "The trouble he had at Paragould almost broke our hearts. In fact, grief over it hastened Monroe's [brother] death."

On Wednesday, December 29, 1909, almost 60 years before the letter was written, a violent winter storm was ripping northern Arkansas. After a day of hunting, brothers John Monroe and James Henry Trammell, both of Greenway in Clay County, Arkansas sought shelter in the Elk Café on Paragould's North Pruett Street.

Advertised as the, "most up-to-date restaurant in northeast Arkansas," the Elk Café served regular and short-order

---

[1] *San Francisco Call*, July 30, 1913.

meals, cigars, liquor and even ice cream. When the brothers entered the café, James quickly became embroiled in an argument with a man identified as Charles Gragg.

A brakeman for the local Iron Mountain and St. Louis Railroad, Gragg had apparently had previous contact with the Trammell boys according to some newspaper reports, but the relationship between James Trammell and Gragg likely ran deeper than previously suspected as it was later reported that Trammell knew Gragg and the he made a joking remark toward Trammell after he passed about paper circulars to those in the café advertising a Memphis saloon he operated.

Whatever the cause, a brief scuffle boiled over, and Trammell jerked his pistol from his side and, while claiming later it was an accident, shot Gragg fatally through the mouth, the *Paragould Daily Press* reported. Trammell immediately fled out the back window of the café and east into the swampy river bottoms east of the city.

He was not seen again for two years.

While no grave has been found in Arkansas or surrounding states for Gragg, research suggests that Gragg had no immediate family except for a sister who lived near Wynne in Cross County at the time of the shooting. However, one news report shows that Oliver Benjamin Gragg of Paragould, identified as 'an uncle' fronted a $50 reward for the capture of Trammell. Yet the full identity of Charles Gragg remains shrouded in mystery and while no grave for Gragg has been located, a recently discovered probate file in Gragg's name was opened two months after his death.

After Trammell fled Paragould in 1909 following the shooting, he first made his way south to Jonesboro where he caught a train at the Frisco Crossing near today's East Nettleton Avenue. From Jonesboro, Trammell went southeast to Memphis, where he then caught a train out west.

Trammell had worked for a time in Memphis as a brakeman for the city's streetcars and it was also variously reported that Trammell operated a saloon in Memphis or, as one newspaper called it, a 'dive.' According to Trammell, he then traveled through Oklahoma City and west through Utah and on to Seattle where he worked for a time as a barber. Apparently not yet feeling safe from the law, Trammell went south to Los Angeles where he claimed to have worked on a ranch and finally to San Francisco where he was employed again as a streetcar motorman under the alias Arthur Hoil.

Initial reports from California show that Trammell and his unnamed wife lived at 1418 Webster Avenue and had arrived in the city in November 1910.

By May 1911, Trammell had become comfortable in his daily routine as a streetcar motorman. At some point, however, Trammell told his wife the sordid details of the shooting affair in Arkansas and acting on the information she alerted the police. Detectives McQuaide and Murphy sat waiting for their man near the Fillmore Street Station at the intersection of Turk Street and as Trammell boarded the street car the detectives followed.

After his arrest and was promptly escorted back to Arkansas by Greene County, Arkansas Sheriff J.D. Lawson. It is believed that during this time, James' brother, John Monroe, who served as Clay County coroner and local druggist, helped fund his brother's travels and exile in the western states. Soon after his arrest in May, the *San Francisco Call* published a detailed interview with Trammell after the told the reporter all that had happened to him since the fatal shooting:

Fugitive Arkansan Ready to Face Trial for Life
Trammell, Living as Hoil, Made Friends Here

LONG SOUGHT SLAYER GLAD CHASE IS OVER

Prisoner Tells Story of Wanderings Since Night of Crime Sixteen Months Ago

J. A. Trammell., the man who confessed Monday to the accidental killing of a man named Gregg [*sic*] in Paragould, Ark. 16 months ago was in a pitiful state of physical and mental collapse in his cell in the central police station last night. After months of wandering from place to place with his wife in a state of suspense and anxiety, uncertain, as he claims, of the nature of his crime, his capture here on Monday night has completely unnerved him. In a voice scarcely above a whisper he tells of his crime and escape… Of his wife he speaks with reluctance and when asked the details of his residence through various parts of the northwest he puffed nervously on his pipe and answered with the reply, "I have forgotten it all… My wife and I never talked of the accident. We knew nothing about it and we did not want to discuss it. I went back for her to my home in Memphis and told her what I had done. She knew all I knew from the first and we had nothing more to say. "When I jumped out of the saloon window in Paragould and ran into the forest I did not know I had killed Gregg [*sic*]. I saw the papers for a few days, but they claimed he was recovering, and after that I heard nothing except indirect rumors until I was arrested…"

"I was never in hiding and while I did not suppose that there were ever detectives on my trail, I was ready at any time to go back. I do not know how the police got the idea that I would flight if caught. I had a chance yesterday to get out of town. I knew they were going to take me. The detectives, Murphy and McQuaide got on my car going uptown and a conductor was put on who told me he was going to relieve me and then the two men got off and took me. I did not have any inclination to run, for, I'll tell you, I was going back on Friday anyway. I don't know how it is coming out back there, but there are 25 men who will testify that I shot Gregg [sic] down in cold blood."

HAGGARD LITTLE MAN Trammel [sic] is a slender little man and yesterday the despair and strain had given him the haggard appearance of a convicted man. His eyes were bloodshot and evasive, his voice was beyond his control and alternated between a husky whisper and a high protesting voice. He punctured every phrase with a pull at his empty pipe and seemed to shrink from contact and the sound of human voices.

"I wish I could have gone back before this game out here." said Trammel [sic] turning his head away. "I was here just long enough, to make friends and I feel humiliated on their account. While I was constantly tortured by the uncertainty of my position, as any man would be, I did my work and lived a normal life with my friends… I had begun to think that I was in no danger and that I might forget it all myself some time. But there were times again when I suffered and it was such a short time ago that I had determined to go back, and then this came. I only hope my brother does not come on I could not see him. I spoke awhile ago of my parents: I have none, but he is father and all the rest to me, and to have had enough humiliation already— I hope he stays away. I wanted to get back and tell the story and square it up for his sake and the sake of my friends, but this throws such a different light on it."

The police say that Trammel [*sic*] was bold and aggressive in his manner last night, but that the contemplation of his possible fate in Arkansas has unmanned him. When alone in his cell, the police say he broke down several times and cried bitterly. Ho brightened up somewhat yesterday when a fellow employee of the United Railroads visited him and as they left Trammel [*sic*] begged his visitor to "send the boys down to see me." From his present manner it would seem that looks forward to conviction as the only possible outcome. When he says, "I do not know how it will turn out." It is not difficult to see how he thinks it will "turn out."

Still, after his return to Paragould, no record of Trammell has been found in the *Greene County Jail Register of Prisoners* and this suggests that he broke free from custody at an early stage in his imprisonment, likely by climbing down the second-floor window with the use of bed sheets which was a common ploy at the time. It seems he knew that as the charge of First Degree Murder had been levied against him in the county's circuit court, he had no other option but to escape again.

After his second flight from Paragould, Trammell was ever seen or heard of again.

John Monroe, who continued his responsible medical duties in northeast Arkansas, probably continued to receive correspondence from James Henry and still supplied funds for his fugitive brother. But what became of him?

Exhaustive research into the life of Trammell has yielded surprising results.

The paper trail of Trammell leads clearly across the Pacific and by 1915, one year after the death of his brother, James Henry Trammell is listed as living at 45 Meagher Street in the heart of Sydney, New South Wales, Australia. Trammell lived on for several more decades down under, the result of which was a first-generation Australian family still thriving today.

In 1929, Trammell helped to break up a fight between the female manage of a wine bar in Manly, a beach-side suburb of Sydney and his dangerous friend Sydney "Tommo" Thompson. While no charges were filed because of the brawl, Thompson lost teeth after the woman threw a padlock at his head.

Trammell worked for many years as a grocer near Sydney Harbour and was even involved in black market crime during World War II. While no evidence shows that Trammell was involved in other, more sinister crimes, he lived in Sydney during a very violent time. Known as the Sydney Razor War, bootleggers and enforcers, known locally as standover men, fought vicious bloody battles on city streets for control of the liquor market and Trammell was surely a witness to this.

Paul Neary, an Australian grandson of James Henry Trammell, confirmed the story of, "A shooting in the south [United States] somewhere." However, details given to the family over the killing of Gragg were inconclusive.

Neary described his grandfather. "He was a very charming man and right until the day he died he maintained his heavy Southern accent. The accent charmed everyone because there were so few Americans living in Australia at that time, especially those from the south. For us grandkids we were always happy to visit because he and my Nan [Phoebe Trammell née Sneedon] always had Coca-Cola in the refrigerator. Also, he would always cook us pancakes for breakfast when we stayed for longer visits. That was not a common breakfast menu for Aussies," said Neary in an interview with the author.

James Trammell died in April 1966 and is buried at Rookwood Cemetery in Rookwood, New South Wales, Australia. Despite the exhaustive story of James Trammell in multiple states and two continents, McQuaide likely did not know the importance of the man whom he arrested that day on the San Francisco streetcar.[2]

---

[2] For more on Trammell see the author's *Main Street Mayhem: Crime, Murder & Justice in Downtown Paragould, 1888-1932* (Tripaw Press, 2016).

eight
Well-Known to Thousands

McQuaide had now been policing the city for decades and had seen numerous and significant changes in San Francisco. A child of Irish immigrants and raised in the slums McQuaide now knew the first women on the police force and was personally responsible for helping to tame the city once known for its bawdy and wild streets.

The *San Francisco Call* reported in July 1911 that McQuaide and his partner Murphy "closed the notorious gambling house conducted by Charley Hamilton under sheriff and brother in law of Finn at 6 Fifth Street. They put the poolroom of Brophy & Collins at Fourth and Mission out of business in short order and made it so hot for "Mother" McGee who ran an opium den at Sixth and Howard streets, that she sold out."[1]

By the 1920s, however, times were changing for the old detective. Criminals once busy with gambling halls, pick-pocketing, and opium dens were now becoming involved in bootlegging and organized crime. In the spring of 1922, police uncovered a crime syndicate whereby jitney (cheap taxi) drivers coalesced to raid a home for its large stash of liquor.

"Sixteen jitney drivers were brought to police headquarters yesterday for questioning," the *San Francisco Chronicle*

---

[1] *San Francisco Call*, July 7, 1911.

reported. "All were subjected to a thorough grilling, but Duncan Matheson, captain of detectives, and Detective Sergeant Arthur McQuaide refused to reveal the result of the interrogation. One of the drivers questioned was a woman."[2]

Documented arrests were reported until 1929. At one point in the mid-1920s, McQuaide was reported as being attached to the San Francisco Police Department's Shotgun Squad, but little evidence of his time with this unit exists.

By the end of World War I in 1918, the department had approximately 930 officers and the lawlessness that characterized the city during the early Gold Rush years began to evolve.

In 1926 McQuaide, now a decades-long veteran of the force, had one more adventure awaiting him. Authorities in London reported that two Austrians, Ludwig and Julius Busch, brothers who had made their residence in San Francisco around 1924, had embezzled over $100,000 from the London branch of the Bank of Italy and the Fidelity and Deposit Company of Maryland. The brothers and the stolen bank bonds were reported missing in their wake.[3]

"The investigators of the bank and the Fidelity company, in which Julius Busch was bonded, determined that the paper was disposed of after it had been taken from his department, and that Ludwig- Busch-may know something of the manner in which it was sold," reported the *Reno Gazette-Journal*.[4]

---

[2] *San Francisco Chronicle*, March 4, 1922.
[3] *Reno Gazette-Journal*, January 30, 1926.
[4] Ibid.

By May it was reported in San Francisco that the wanted brothers had been found that that McQuaide was on his way to London to collect his prisoners. "McQuaide will first go to Sacramento where he will get the signature of Governor Richardson for extradition papers. Then he will go to Washington, New York, and London… He will begin his return as soon as the prisoners are placed in his care."[5]

Policemen like McQuaide experienced brutal Chinatown Tong Wars and into the 1920s with the purging of liquor during prohibition. The Tong Wars were eventually resolved with a primitive style of community policing, which would eventually become the department's ruling philosophy. Under police Chief O'Brien, Inspector Jack Manion brought Chinatown leaders together, and persuaded the tong leaders to sign an agreement ending the violence.

The era of Prohibition which lasted from 1920 to 1933, provided a unique example of law enforcement dealing with a virtually unenforceable law. The liquor laws were brazenly violated by everyone looking to disrupt law and order and for people like McQuaide, drinkers of liquor or not, the law stood to be enforced one way or another regardless of personal opinions.

Following his departure from the police, sometime after 1929, few details remain about the life of McQuaide. On Sunday, January 1, 1939, the same day future technology giant Hewlett-Packard was founded in Palo Alto, California, Arthur McQuaide died. The next day the *San Francisco Chronicle* ran a brief obituary on page 11.

> Inspector Arthur McQuaide, 68, veteran of 40 years' service with the San Francisco Police Department, died

---

[5] *San Francisco Chronicle*, May 5, 1926.

suddenly last night, following a stroke at Sixth and Market streets.

A native of San Francisco, McQuaide formed the first auto detail, and at the time of his death was well known to thousands as a member of the check detail of the detective bureau.

He joined the department in 1898, rose to corporal in 1910 and sergeant in 1915. He was attached to the inspectors' bureau since 1906 and was the oldest member in point of service in the detective bureau.

McQuaide lived at 521 Post Street.[6]

McQuaide died alone for his wife passed away in 1919 and the couple had no children. Despite the aged detective's bravery and commitment to law and order he remains just another forgotten piece of San Francisco history.

---

[6] *San Francisco Chronicle*, January 2, 1939.

appendix I

Criminal slang from circa 1890-1920. Courtesy of *HistoricalCrimeDetective.com*

A

A beef stew singer—A bad soloist.
A boost—-Talking for the interests.
A bum lamp—A bad eye.
A bum mit—A sore arm or crippled hand.
A bum steer—False information or direction.
A bundle—Package from home; a woman; a roll of greenbacks.
A cheap thief—One who steals from churches.
A cold meat party—A wake.
A crimp—Runner for sailors' boarding house.
A fairy—A young girl.
A fall guy—One who assumes blame to shield others.
A flat joint worker—-An assistant crooked gambler.
A flat wheel—A crippled leg or foot.
A flat worker—One who steals from dwellings.
A flying jib—A talkative drunk.
A four-flusher—A bluffer, a braggart.
A full—An arrest.
A good fellow—Thief who spends freely and pays bills promptly.
A green goods man—One who sells worthless securities or bogus money.
A gridler—An English street singer.
A gun moll—A woman pickpocket.

A hum shaft—A bad leg [*bum* written above]
A hunch—A tip; a presentiment.
A jolt—Doing time in prison.
A knock—Talking against the interests.
A lift—A help.
A lunger—Consumptive.
A mizzen mast worker—A top-story thief.
A moll buzzer—A thief who robs women only.
A nerver—A dead-head. One who gets in or who is passed by without paying.
A panhandler—A beggar.
A pig—Thief's prostitute.
A pin-head—A dumb fellow or a know-nothing.
A quality gentleman—A man of birth and refinement.
A rag—A woman.
A rumble—A noise or outcry from the victim.
A skirt—A woman.
A smart fellow—A thief who makes a good haul and escapes arrest.
A sosh on—Drunk.
A square head—A Swede.
A stool pigeon—Thief who informs on others for protection.
A sure thing gambler—One who bets with suckers at races and steals.
A swell booster—Successful female shoplifter.
A swell mob—Gang of thieves with money and clothes.
A swell mouth—A first class lawyer.
A title tapper—One who raises money on forged deeds.
A trusty—Convict who carries tales to authorities.
A valentine—A short jail sentence.
A Willie boy—An effeminate man; submerged manhood.
Alias—A false name.

All to the good—All right, gained.
Alley rat—Thief who robs persons in alleys.
Anchor—To Stop.
Angel—A person with money, one easily cheated.
Arithmetic dog—Crippled dog, who puts down some legs and carries others.
Auntie—Keeper of assignation house.

B

Bad dough—Counterfeit money.
Badger—One man blackmailing another caught in a compromising position with his mistress.
Bad—Good.
Baldy—An old man.
Bandwagon—The majority; the crowd; successful ones.
Bang up—-Done right; good; red handed; without warning.
Barker—Auctioneer; street or sidewalk solicitor.
Baron—Hotel beat.
Bats—Delirium tremens.
Batter—To knock on back door; to beg; to solicit.
Beak—A magistrate; a judge.
Beanery—A cheap restaurant.
Beat—To escape; to defraud; to overcome.
Beefer—A complaining or informing person.
Beef—To holler; complain; to tell;
Belched—Told it; informed; gave up information.
Benjamin—Overcoat.
Benny wooden—A coffin.
Benny—An overcoat.
Bested—An advantage; overcome.
Betsy—Fist, weapon.

Big house—Penitentiary.
Big mitt—Crooked gambler.
Bilked—Fooled, evaded.
Bit—A term in prison; a share of the spoils.
Black Maria—Wagon for hauling purposes.
Blackie—Person with dark hair; surname for a crook with black hair.
Blackmail—A woman decoys a man and her alleged husband demands a fee for injury to his peace of mind.
Blackstone—A judge.
Blanket mortgage—A conveyance to defraud creditors.
Blanket stiff—A western tramp.
Blew in—Came in; came to town.
Blind baggage—Front end of a baggage car with no doors.
Blind—A make-believe; a stall; a pretense; an excuse.
Blink—No good.
Block—A watch; to oppose; to head off; to stop; human head.
Bloke—Another person; a dumb fellow.
Bloomer—A failure.
Blowed-in-the-glass—A trustworthy pal; professional; a fact.
Blowing a peter—Blowing open a safe.
Blowing—Spending freely; treating; leaving a place.
Blow—To tell around; to leave a place; to let alone.
Bo—A fellow man; a tramp; being short for hobo.
Board stiff—Walking advertisement.
Bobbed up—Appeared; came in; heard from.
Bobby—An English policeman.
Body snatcher—Undertaker.
Boil up—A hobo washes clothes and himself by a camp fire.
Boiled dinner—An Irishman; a New England meal.

Boiled out—After visiting Hot Springs for baths.
Boiled shirt—A soft shirt.
Boilermaker—A lover.
Boiling up—Stopping at water to wash clothes, etc.
Bolt—To leave in haste; to oppose.
Bones—Dice.
Bonnet—A hat; a sky piece; a lid.
Booby Hatch—City jail.
Booked—Registered at a police station.
Booster—A shoplifter.
Bootleg—Sell or carry liquor against law.
Booze—Liquor.
Boozer—Drunkard.
Bouncer—One who keeps order in the house; private officer.
Bowl of suds—Glass of beer.
Bowling up—Drinking up.
Box man—Safe blower.
Bracelets—Handcuffs.
Brace—To beg; to ask; a combination.
Brass up—Divide the spoils.
Brass—Nerve.
Break away—Separate; to leave.
Brich—Front trouser pocket.
Brief—Pawn ticket.
Broke a leg—Got arrested.
Broke—Without means.
Brush—Whiskers.
Buck—A priest; a male black man; a dollar; to oppose.
Bucket Shop—Where stocks are sold but not delivered; a gambling den.
Buddy—A companion.
Bug house—Insane asylum.

Buggy—Insane.
Bull buster—One who assaults policemen.
Bull con—Untruth; false information ; fictitious story.
Bull Pen—Police hold-over.
Bull—A policeman.
Bum rocks—Diamonds with flaws in them.
Bum Steer—Wrong direction; false information.
Bunco—To rob; to cheat.
Bunger—Discolored eye.
Buried—Convicted; cheated; hid.
Burr head—A black person.
Bust—A blow; a strike.
Buster—A burglar's tools; a fighter.
Butt in—Getting into conversation without invitation.
Button—A poison used to kill dogs.
Buzz the Rube—To converse with the victim or the one unaware of the plot.
Buzzard—A chief of police; a mean person.

C

C.A. coat—Coat with slits to hold begged food.
Cadet—An enticer of young girls.
Cadger—Trickster; beggar.
Call down—A reprimand.
Call the turn—To identify person, or see through a deal incomplete.
Can—Bottom; backside (butt).
Candy kid—Fair haired boy with woman.
Canned—To get discharged; arrested.
Cannon—Gun; a pick-pocket.
Can—Police station.
Canuck—A French-Canadian.
Capper—Go-between for gamblers; fakirs; encourager.

Card—A playing card folded as a pouch containing opium.
Casa—House.
Case note—Dollar bill.
Caunfort Ladron—Head of a gang of thieves; master thief.
Central office—Police headquarters.
Chalked—Cell marked with chalk; thieves' marks for personal information.
Charlie Adams—A Yankee jail.
Cheap—Mean; stingy; economical.
Check kiting—Dating ahead checks and expecting to have money to meet same.
Cheesy—Bad.
Cheroo—Quit; warning of a confederate.
Chew the rag—To talk.
Chew—To eat.
Chi—Chicago.
Chicken feed—Small change.
Chink—Chinaman; money.
Chip damper—A money till.
Chippy—A young woman of doubtful character.
Chivy—A face.
Chuck—Food.
Chuck—Meals.
Church hypocrite—One who steals while he prays.
Cinch—A certainty.
Cincie—Cincinnati.
Clam—An easy mark; quiet.
Clouting—Stealing at night; assaulting.
Cluck—Counterfeit coin.
Cockroaches playing marbles— Tumbling bugs rolling up their eggs in cow manure.
Codger—An old man.

Cod—Tantalize; a joke.
Coffin nails—Cigarettes.
Coffin varnish—Bad whiskey.
Coke head—A user of Cocaine.
Coke or moker—A user of Cocaine.
Cold feet—Lost courage.
Cold one—Dead; no value; bottle of beer worth drinking.
Collared—Arrested.
Come back—A complaint; a reply; response; detected; discovery, etc.
Come on—A sucker; a mark; an enticer.
Come-along—A tool for forcing a safe.
Coming home—Released from prison.
Con—Conductor; falsity; lie; a convict; consumption.
Cooler—A cell.
Cop a heal—To sneak upon
Cop the coin—Steal the money.
Copped out—Arrested; stole; prevented from being counted.
Copper—Policeman.
Coppers—Tonsils.
Cop—Policeman; steal.
Cough—To tell.
Cove—A fellow.
Cracker—A poor Southerner.
Cracking—Speaking about; forcing; an attempt.
Crapper—State prison; toilet.
Creeper—Woman who steals from drunks; sneak thief; rubber shoe.
Crib—A saloon; house of prostitution; joint; hang out.
Critter fiend—Horse thief.
Croaker—One who kills.
Croak—To die.

Crocus—A doctor.
Crook—One who makes a living without work, dishonest.
Croppie—A corpse.
Cross lots—Over country; avoiding roads.
Crumb—A louse.
Crumbed up—Full of lice.
Crush—A crowd.
Cush—Money.
Cuter—The prosecuting attorney.
Cutting—Division of the spoils.

D

D. and S.—Dangerous and suspicious.
Daffy—Demented; insane.
Dame—A girl.
Damp powder—Not to be feared; fake agitator.
Damper—Money drawer.
Darb—Money.
Date—An appointment.
Dead one—Person without means.
Deck hand—A domestic.
Derby—A good haul.
Derrick—A shoplifter.
Dicer—A hat.
Dick—Detective; sheriff; criminal publication; The Detective.
Dinge—A black person.
Dip—A pick-pocket.
Dippy—Insane; crazy.
Disciples—Jury.
Ditch—To leave; to cast away; to abandon; get left; hide; sidetracked.
Diver—A pick-pocket.

Divorced—Temporarily separated by court action.
Doe—An infant.
Dogged—Followed.
Dog—Sausage.
Doing a bit—Serving time in prison.
Doing time—Serving time in prison.
Doniker—Prison cell toilet.
Dope—Information; medicine; drugs; narcotics.
Dorf—German village.
Doss house—A lodging house.
Doss—Bed; asleep.
Double crossed—To betray confidence; fooled.
Doubled up—Got married.
Dough—Money.
Douse the glim—Put out the light.
Douse—To extinguish.
Down and out—In needy circumstances.
Down below—Penitentiary.
Drag—Horse and wagon; burglar's tool; political influence; draw of smoke from pipe, cigarette or cigar.
Dress suit burglar—Lobbyist; slippery fellow; smooth person.
Dressed in—To prepare for prison sentence; being measured, photographed, haircut, and donned with prison uniform.
Dressed out—To receive discharge; suit money, etc., when leaving prison.
Drop of hat—Quick.
Duck—A pail; an object used for signal.
Ducket—A ticket.
Duck—To leave; to dodge; to sneak away.
Dummy—Bread.
Dump—Hang out; low resort.

Dump—Place; city, town or burg.
Dungeon—Dark cell.

Durry Nacker—A German female hawker (a sales person who shouts).
Dust—Money; to run away.

E
Ease—To rob.
Easy money—A certainty; money made without physical effort.
Elbow—Fly cop; a detective.

F
Fagin—Thief; a person who teaches others how to steal.
Fall back—A friend; money or re-sources to use in case of need.
Fall Guy—Thief who takes blame and penalty to save pals.
Fall money—A fund maintained by thieves for their protection.
Fan—To locate pocketbook; to feel one's way; to inquire; to search.
Fence—A receiver of stolen property.
Fill in—To become one of the party; no active part.
Fillings—Food.
Fine as silk—In good condition.
Finger prints—An ink impression of the finger tips used for identification.
Finger—An officer of the law.
Finks—Drunks.
First degree—Arrest.
Fixed—Bribed; bought; pre-arranged.
Flag—To stop.

Flash—A roll of money, real on the outside, small amount inside; a look.
Flat joint—Crooked gambling joint.
Flatties—Policemen that walk beats.
Flatty—Police officer who walks a beat.
Flim-flammer—Short change operator.
Flip—Too forward; too outspoken.
Floater—A traveler; a tramp.
Flop—To stop; lie down; rest.
Flossie—A Blonde.
Flounder—A person from Newfoundland.
Flush—With plenty of money.
Fly Cop—A detective.
Focused—Looked.
Four flusher—One who acts for effect.
Frame up—Pre-arranged affair.
Free board—In jail.
Freeze—Retain; to keep.
French leave—Escape.
Fresh Fish—A new hand; a newcomer.
Frisk—A search.
Front Office—Office of Chief of Police or Chief of Detectives.
Front—A showing, good clothes.
Full up—All needed.

G
Gab—Talk.
Gaff—Punishment.
Gag—Any begging trick; any old game of fraud or cheat.
Gall—Cheek; brazen; forwardness.
Gallways—Whiskers.
Galway—A Catholic priest.

Game—Courageous; full of courage; perseverance.
Garbage joint—A cheap restaurant.
Garroter—A robber who strangles and uses force.
Gas meter—Valise.
Gash—A fast woman.
Gassy—Talkative.
Gat—Revolver.
Gay cat—One who gets information, for robbers by selling trinkets in places.
Gazaboo—An unknown man.
Gentleman burglar—A well-dressed burglar.
Gerver—Safe blower.
Get away—Successful escape; retreat.
Get on the outside of something—To eat.
Getting by—Missed but not molested; living without work; not detected.
Giggers—Guards.
Gilhooley—A fool.
Ginny—An Italian woman.
Giving up—Paying for protection; dividing; giving information.
Glad hand—A hand shake without and real friendship.
Glad Mitt—Warm welcome; a helping hand institution similar to Salvation Army.
Glim Grafter—Fake Optician.
Glims—Eyes; spectacles; light.
Glims—Spectacles.
Glorie—Business.
Goat—Resources; a factional politician.
Goats—Farmers.
Gob—Mouth.
Gofer—Safe, with time lock.
Going out—Prisoner's release.

Goldie—A surname applied to a person with light hair.
Goniff—Jewish word for pickpocket.
Gonner—Convicted.
Goods—Money; stolen stuff; spoils; incriminating evidence.
Gooseberry—A line of clothes.
Gopherman—Safe blower.
Gopher—Time vault.
Gorilla—A thief who uses violence.
Graft—Dishonest money; something easy.
Gran—Leg; an old person.
Gravel train—Go between of Lobbyists who buy up legislators.
Gravy—Easy.
Greased—Paid.
Grease—Nitroglycerine.
Grease—To pay for protection; pay tribute.
Greasy coat thief—Pickpocket who steals only enough for beer and hangs
out in bar rooms.
Grifter—con artist, swindler.
Grit—The road; to steal.
Grub—Food.
Guff—Worthless talk.
Gull—Victim.
Gummer—Turnkey.
Gum—Rubber hose used for beating prisoners.
Gumshoeworker—Private detective
Gun maker—One who teaches boys and girls to become thieves.
Gun—A thief; pickpocket.
Gunning—With gun in pocket looking for an enemy.
Guy—To tease; a man; a stranger.

H

Halter—Hangman's noose.
Hand me down—A ready-made suit of clothes.
Hand out—Begged food given in response to an appeal of hunger.
Handle—Nose.
Happy dust—Cocaine.
Hard stuff—Gold and silver.
Harness bull—Uniform officer.
Harnessed box—A safe with extra bars or protection in front.
Harp—An Irishman.
Hash slinger—Waiter; restaurant worker.
Hasher—Waiter.
Hay rack—Cell bed.
Head light—Diamond stud; a whiskey nose.
Heat on—Drunk.
Heeler—A politician in a ward, called a ward heeler; a bouncer.
Heel-—Sneak thief.
Heifer—A woman.
Hep—To be aware; to catch on.
Herring—A British subject.
Hike—Walk.
Hiney—German.
Hinky Dink's—Clark Street, Chicago; a resort in Chicago.
Hip—Wise, aware of.
Hitting the grit—Traveling.
Hitting the pipe—Smoking opium.
Hitting the pot—Drinking out of a can.
Hitting the road—Traveling.
Hitting the stem—Smoking opium.
Hobo—Tramp.

Hock shop—Pawnbroker's store.
Hock—Pawner. To pawn something.
Hog box—A crooked faro box.
Hoister—Shoplifter, one who steals in stores, from counters, etc.
Hole with rings around—Doughnut.
Holler—A complaint.
Home guard—Resident of the town.
Honey—A black person.
Hoof—The foot.
Hoof—Walk.
Hooligan—A bum; an English loafer or hoodlum.
Hoop—A ring.
Hop joint—Place where opium is smoked.
Hop scotching—Crossing the country and avoiding the main traveled roads.
Hop talk—Bragging; exaggeration; talk without facts.
Hop—Opium.
Hoppers—Hotel bell boys.
Hoppy—A cripple.
Hops—Tea; beer.
Hot air—Senseless talk.
Hot coppers—Dry throat; recovering from a drunk.
Hot foot—Run.
Hot—Stolen in town; being looked for; reported stolen.
Hounded—Persecuted.
Hours—Time given a person by the authorities to leave the city.
Houseman—A burglar.
Hunch—Presentiment; a tip.
Hunk—Revenge.
Hustler—A prostitute who solicits business on the streets.

I

Icy mitt—The shake from a sweetheart.
In limbo—Doing time in jail.
Inmate—A prostitute who works in a brothel.
In quad—In jail.
In trouble—In jail; a charge against him.
Irish club house—Police station.
Irish slum—Cheap jewelry that tarnishes in a short time.
Italian hand—An unseen force.

J

Jabber—Pugilist.
Jacob—A ladder.
Jagged—Intoxicated; drunk.
Jail arithmetic—Making up a false list of expenses to cover up embezzlement.
Jane—A female.
Jap—A Japanese person.
Jar—To surprise; to compel.
Jarvie—Vest Pocket.
Java—Coffee.
Jeans—Pants, trousers.
Jerried—Hurt; injured.
Jersey lightning—Bad whiskey.
Jim Crow car—A car for black people only.
Jimmie a bull—To stop or kill a policeman.
Jimmy—A bar with a crook in it so as to produce leverage.
JoBaJoo—Freight train.
Jobbed—Prearranged unjustly convicted.
Jobs put over—Crimes committed.
John Bater—A victim; a sucker.
John O'Brien—Irish stew; a freight train.

Johnnie yegg—A tramp safe blower.
Johnnie—One who enjoys the company of women.

Joint—Meeting house for thieves; resort where liquor is sold.
Jollier—A flatterer.
Jolly—To flatter.
Jolts—-Years in prison.
Josh—To joke; ridicule; to make fun of; a country person.
Jug—A jail; a safe; building where money is kept.
Jugged—Arrested.
Jungle—Prison.
Jungles—Woods or brush outside of city limits.
Junk—Bogus jewelry; worthless paraphernalia.

K
Keister—Satchel; grip; valise; bag; a safe.
Kettle—Watch.
Kiann—A mixed breed dog.
Kick—A complaint.
Kicks—Shoes.
Kid—An infant; a joke; a tease.
Kidder—-A joker.
Kike—A worthless or unsuccessful Jew thief.
Kipp—Lodging house.
Kip—Sleep.
Kirk—Church.
Kisser—The mouth; the face.
Kite out—Drunk.
Kite—An immoral woman.
Knob—The head.
Knocker—One who speaks against the interests of another.
Knockout drops—A drug used to stupefy.
Knowledge box—A school.

L

Lace curtains—Whiskers.
Lambster—A fugitive.
Lamb—To run.
Lathered up—A safe's cracks soaped shut, ready to put in the nitro.
Law ghost—A lawyer who never appears in court, but prepares cases for trial, looking up law, etc.
Lay out—Gambling outfit; opium outfit; an illegal collection.
Laying on the side—Smoking opium.
Laying out—Assaulting.
Laying paper—Passing worthless checks, drafts, etc.
Leather—Purse.
Leeping—Effect of cocaine on the eyes.
Leery—Afraid; doubtful of.
Lemon pool—Two playing against one in a game of pool; beat at pool by two confederates.
Lemon—One's nose; nothing; a fake.
Life boat—A pardon.
Life saver—Drink of whiskey.
Lingo—Foreign language.
Lip—Talk. Back-talk.
Live wire—Active person, tiling or place.
Lobster—A slow person; one without much intelligence; unsuccessful.
Log cabin—A saloon.
Lost a man—One of the gang arrested while in operation.
Louse House—Cheap boarding house.
Lover—Supported by the wages of sin or by a fallen woman; a pimp.
Lusher—A hard drinker.

M

Maced—Asked; begged.
Mack—A lover.
Madam—Keeper of house of ill repute.
Main bull—Chief of police or detectives.
Main guy—Head person.
Main squeeze—A head fellow.
Main stem—Principal thoroughfare.
Make one—To recognize; to identify.
Marble Heart—Cold reception; no attention; deaf ear.
Mark—An easy person.
Marks or Merits—Behavior record in prison.
Marquereaux—Pimp.
Marys—Prison Missioners.
Masher—A loafer who tries to force his acquaintance on women.
Measured—Signalized by the Bertillon system.
Meat Cleaver—Knife.
Meat wagon—Body; hearse.
Merchant—One that runs a shell game.
Mission stiff—A missionary; a convert.
Mitt—Hand.
Mixed—A fight.
Mixed-ale philosopher—A drunken speaker.
Mizzen Mast Worker—Top story burglar.
Mob—A gang of pickpockets.
Mob—A number of persons banded together for the purpose of stealing.
Moll Buzzer—One who robs women only.
Moll—A prostitute; a woman.
Moniker—A name; an alias.
Moonlighter—A midnight prowler.

Moonshiner—One who makes whiskey and pays no government tax.
Mouthpiece—A lawyer.
Mr. Bates—Victim.
Mr. Marks—Victim.
Mug—To photograph; the face; an Irishman; a photograph.
Mum—Silence.
Mush fake—One who mends umbrellas and wash tubs, etc.
Mush—An umbrella.
Musser—A fighter; a bully.

N

Nabbed—Arrested.
Nancy—An effeminate man.
Necktie Party—A hanging.
Nickel movement—Five cent or cheap whiskey.
Nickel snatcher—Conductor or cashier.
Nick—Steal.
Nifty—Show temper; contrary.
Nipped—Stolen; arrested.
Nippers—Handcuffs.
Nix—No; stop it.
Nose warmer—Short stemmed pipe.
Notch house—House of prostitution.
Notch Moll—A female inmate of a house of prostitution.
Notches on gun—Number of men killed.
Nuck—Thief.
Number two—A shovel.
Nut College—Insane asylum.
Nut head—Crazy man.
Nut squealers—Men working the shell game.

Nut—Plead.
Nutty—Insane.

O

Office man—Officer from police headquarters.
Office—Signal; recognition; cue.
Oil—Nitroglycerine.
Old Gazabe—Old man.
Oliver—Moon.
On the gun—Picking pockets for a living.
On the hog—Financially embarrassed ; broke; beating way about the country.
On the hummer—Financially embarrassed ; broke; beating way about the country.
On the quiet—Forcing a safe without the use of explosives.
On the turf—Prostituting streetwalker; inmate of house of prostitution.
On the water wagon—Not drinking.
One spot—A dollar bill.
Outsiders—An instrument for turning keys from the outside.

P

Pad money—Money to pay for one's lodging.
Paddy—Padlock; an Irishman.
Pan handler—A beggar.
Panel worker—Male or female who rob persons after enticing them into a room.
Panhandlers' heaven—A locality where the natives are liberal to beggars.
Parole—Conditional release from prison.
Peach—To inform; a good one.

Peeler—Irish policeman.
Pencil pusher—Clerk.
Penny-weighter—Jewelry thief.
Pen—Penitentiary; state or Government prison.
Pensy—Pennsylvania.
Pete—A safe.
Peter man—A safe blower.
Petered out—Tired; worn out.
Phiz—Face.
Phoney—A substitute; bogus; not real.
Picking flowers from century plants—Not working.
Pick-up—Arrested accidentally without any specific charge.
Pig—A prostitute.
Piker—A lounger; to view without paying; busybody.
Pike—To look at; to view; the road.
Pill—A portion of opium rolled into a ball and ready to be cooked and smoked.
Pinched—Arrested.
Pipe-dream—Something not real; idealistic idea.
Piped—Watched.
Pipe—To look at; something sure; something easy.
Planted—Hid; saved; buried.
Plant—To bide; a hiding place for stolen goods.
Plater—One who breaks glass windows to steal.
Plucked—Robbed.
Plugger—One who encourages you to enter a game of chance.
Poacher—Tramp; sheep thief; one who does not work.
Poke out—Begged food or sandwich ; a lunch or food handed out the back door.
Poke—Pocket-book.
Polio—Postoffice.

Political pauper—No good in politics anymore; poor politician.
Politsiti—A warning.
Porch climber—Thief who gains entrance by climbing up a porch.
Pork dump—A poor place to stay; poor boarding house.
Pot slinger—Cook, kitchen help.
Poteen—Irish whiskey.
Pound the ear—Sleep.
Pratt leather—Pocket book carried in hip pocket.
Pratt—Stealing pocket-books from hip pockets.
Pressing brick for the city—Walking around; doing nothing.
Props—Diamonds or other jewelry
Prowlers—Plain clothes officers or men.
Psalm singer—A trusty; an informer in prison.
Puff—An explosive.
Puffed up—Mad; proud; elevated opinion of one's self.
Puffer—One who boasts or speaks in exaggeration.
Puffin rod—A revolver.
Pug—A pugilist.
Punk boy—A boy trained by tramps to steal for them.
Punk—Bread.
Push—Associates with; crowd.

Q

Queer—Counterfeit money.
Queered—Forestalled; prevented; stopped; informed on.

R

Rag—Handkerchiefs; dress; a woman; paper money; a flag.
Rams—Farmers.

Rank—No good; strong; without concealment.
Rapper—One who tells; testifies; complains; or prosecutes.
Rattler—Freight train.
Raven—A message.
Red eye—Whiskey.
Reef a leather—To raise the lining of a pocket in order to get out a pocketbook.
Reported—A voluntary visit of a thief on arrival in town to the office of the chief of police.
Rep—Reputation.
Right—One who protects thieves, and trusted by them.
Ringer—An exact duplicate.
Ripped—Lots of stealing.
River Rat—A river thief; one who hangs out at a river.
Rocks—Diamonds.
Rocq soup—A kettle of hot water.
Rod—Revolver.
Rods—Iron supports under a car.
Roll—Currency in a roll; fund of money; a stake.
Romped-on—Arrested; slugged; detained.
Room—A cell.
Rough house—Fight; carousal; disorder; confusion.
Rough neck—A bully, rough fellow; fighter.
Rounding to—Confessing; informing.
Roust-about—Laborer with no settled home; steamboat laborer.
Rubberneck—An inquisitive person.
Rube—A farmer; an easy person;, stranger in town.
Run in—Arrested.
Runner—Messenger; informer.
Rustler—Horse or cattle thief—western thieves.

S

Sailing—Listening.
Sails—Ears.
Salt Creek—Death; executed; gone forever.
Salve—A patronizing talk; con-talk; bogus tales; inducements.
Salve—Smooth talk.
Sawdust—Dynamite; saloon in a mining town; circus arena.
Scenery—Clothes.
Scoff house—Eating place.
Scoff—Eating hastily; without manners.
Scot free—Escaped; with no restraint.
Scratcher—Forger.
Screw—A tool; a key; the jailor or turnkey; go away.
Screw—Turnkey; to leave.
Scouting—Fugitive, avoiding certain locations.
Scrub squad—Sanitary gang in prison.
Selling platter—Small store; poor race horse.
Set down—A square meal.
Settled—Sentenced to prison.
Shabang—A poor house.
Shack—A poor house; A small cabin to live in.
Shadowed—Followed; kept track of; actions noted.
Shaneen—An Irish upstart.
Shark hunter—A thief looking for drunken men to rob.
Shark—Money lender.
Sheeney—A Jew; a Hebrew; a stingy person.
Sheet—Register at hotel or police station.
Shine—A black person.
Shiner—A black eye.
Shook down—Made to give up money for protection or information. (Shake down).

Shooting a jug—Blowing a safe.
Shorts—Transfer point on short runs of a street R. R.
Shovel stiff—Laborer with a shovel.
Shoving the queer—Passing counterfeit money.
Shy—Short.
Shyster—A no good lawyer who does small and mean things.
Side door sleeper—A box car.
Silvertop—A light haired person.
Sinkers—Doughnuts.
Sixer—Six months.
Sizzorbill—A long legged man; a farmer.
Skates on—Drunk.
Skee—Whiskey.
Skidoo—Leave; go; same as "23." (23 Skidoo)
Skunk—A mean person.
Sky pilot—Minister of the gospel.
Sky-blue—Vegetable soup.
Sky—Short.
Slack—Back talk; response.
Slag—Watch chain.
Slats—Ribs.
Slave—Servant.
Sleep Hollow—A New Jersey Prison.
Slinging the lingu—Talking in a foreign tongue.
Slob—An easy, unkempt person; an ignoramus.
Slobbing—Kissing.
Slop—Stale beer.
Sloughworker—Thief who robs country houses.
Slow grafter—Day light burglar.
Slugged—Assaulted; waylaid.
Slum—Cheap jewelry.
Smoke wagon—Revolver.

Smoked—Shot at.
Sneeze wagon—Automobile.
Snide—Mean; cheap.
Snitch—One who tells.
Snow—Cocaine.
Snuffed—Killed.
Soaking—Placing in pawn; hitting.
Soakville—Pawnshop.
Sounding—Locating a man's pocket book.
Soup—A concoction made by boiling dynamite in water and then drawing off the bottom, which is nitroglycerine, used for safe-blowing.
Spark—Diamond.
Speak easy—A joint; illegal bar room.
Spiel—A talk.
Spieler—Cheap lawyer.
Spieling—Talking; walking; waltzing.
Spike Hennessy—An old-fashioned method of safe blowing; using gunpowder.
Spiked—Stopped; prevented; soda water or other drink containing whiskey.
Spill—Terminus; transfer point of a R. R.
Spliced—Married.
Split—A division of spoils.
Sponging—Accepting, without returning, hospitality.
Spotted—Detected; seen.
Spot—Term given to a year in prison; one spot, one year; two spot is two years, etc; waiting, meeting or viewing a place.
Spring—Liberate.
Sprouter—A fluent speaker.
Squalks—Sings.
Squawks

Square box—An honest faro dealing box, wherein a player has a chance.
Squared—Making good a loss; arranged so there will be no prosecution.
Staking—Assisting financially; giving; loaning.

Stall—Something to divert attention ; one who assists pickpockets.
Stand pat—Being firm; refusing to give up information.
Star boarder—One who enjoys all the privileges; one with financial backing.
Stash—Hide.
State—Tobacco furnished by the state.
Steamed grub—Prison fare.
Steer—Direction; information.
Steerer—Pilot for a gang of thieves; grafter.
Stickers—Postage stamps.
Sticks—Woods, timber.
Stick—To remain; to wait.
Stick-up—A highway man or robbery.
Stiff—An old person; a dead person.
Stir—Penitentiary.
Stir-simple—A lack of reason; dullness caused by long confinement in prison.
Stone jug—A prison built of stone.
Stood out—Taken out of line in prison for violating the rules.
Stood up—Stood up in line with other thieves for identification.
Stool Pigeon—A thief who gives officers information about other thieves.
Stowaway—Hid away on a carrier to avoid paying fare; a politician on a padded administration payroll.

Strads—Trousers.
Stretch—A term in prison.
String 'em—Fool them.
Strings and Bonnets—Fuses and caps used by safe blowers.
Strong-arm—Robbed by force.
Struck—Impressed; fascinated.
Struck—Measured by the Bertillon system.
Student—One on the administration payroll who does not work.
Suds—Beer.
Summer boarder—One who stays a short time and acts foolish and queer.
Sure-thing man—A crooked gambler.
Swag—Stolen property.
Sweat box—An imaginary steam heated box used by the police to force confessions from prisoners. In reality it is a series of crossfire questions and confusing questions.
Swell mob—Expert pickpocket.
Swig—A drink.
Swipe—Steal.
Switch—Transferring; passing to another; substituting.

T

Tab—Check; to keep track of or account of, (keep tabs on).
Tailed—Followed by a detective.
Tall Sticks—Woods.
Tanking up—Drinking.
Tart—A girl of questionable character.
Terrier—An Irishman.
Thimble rigger—A swindler at the shell game.
Third degree—A violent method of the police to coerce a confession or gain information.

Third rail—A pickpocket on a R. R.
Throwed down—Betrayed.
Tinker—A bungler.
Tip your mitt—Make known your purpose; exposed.
Tip—A warning ; advance knowledge.
To the hay—To bed.
To the sheets—To bed.
Toad skins—Paper money.
Togged up—Dressed up.
Togs—Clothes.
Tommy buster—A man who beats prostitutes and lewd women.
Tommy—A girl of questionable character.
Tool—One of a gang of pickpockets who does the actual stealing.
Top-piece—Reward. Hat.
Touch—A theft by pocket picking.
Tout—One who gives supposed advance knowledge of race returns.
Track 13 and a washout—A term in a western prison.
Trader—A prostitute.
Tribunal—Court.
Trimmer—Cheat, fraud.
Trolly—An improvised carrier for notes, etc., in prison.
Tub—Glass of beer.
Turn a trick—A theft accomplished.
Turned out—Released from prison; enter on a career of crime.
Turnip—A watch.
Twenty-three—An invitation to leave; originated in New Orleans, La.
Twist—Waltz.

U

Uncle—A prefix to the name of pawnbroker.
Under cover—In hiding; of reserved intentions, or thought.
Underground wires—Persons in public life who quietly secure a prisoner's release.
Unfortunate—Arrested, tried and convicted.
Up the river—Sentenced to Sing Sing, a New York prison.
Use the wax—To take an impression of a key.

V

Vag—A vagrant; person with no means of support; charge used by the police on account of meaning most any misdemeanor.
Velvet—Easy.
Vestry thief—A conman who works in churches.
Vise—To be aware of what is transpiring.
Vugged—Convicted of vagrancy.

W

Walk the plank—Shown up to a collection of officers.
Wedged in—Put in same cell to secure information.
Weed—Tobacco; to separate the good from the bad.
Welcher—One who informs; a quitter.
Wet Goods—Stolen Goods.
Wharf rat—One who steals around the wharves on the river front.
Whiskers—City magistrate.
Whiskey tenor—A bad soloist.
White mule—Alcohol.
White stuff—Morphine.
Whop—Less than thirty days in prison.
Wienie—A sausage; loaf of bread.

Windjammer—A talkative person.
Window—Spectacles.
Windy—Profuse conversation.
Wing—An arm; section of prison; to shoot in the arm.
Wingy—A person with one arm.
Wipe—A handkerchief.
Wirepuller—Diplomat.
Wood—A policeman's billy club.
Woody—To go mad; insane.
Working—Operating; stealing.
Wrong—Not to be trusted by thieves; an honest man.

Y

Yap—An easy victim.
Yegg—Tramp thieves; safe blowers.
Yenshee—Residue left in the pipe after smoking opium, which is boiled over
again and smoked.

appendix II

Arthur McQuaide's record of known arrests

- Unknown date – W.R. Hopson of Omaha, Nebraska on charges of "worthless mining certificates". McQuaide nabbed the wrong Hopson and the man was released.
- September 1901 – Charles Barrett, bunco artist arrested while trying to swindle victim Nels Anderson along Ninth Street near Howard.
- April 1902 – Willis McKnight, W. Johnson, arrested on charges of robbery.
- December 1904 – Henry E. Wisherd, arrested after attempting to rob a woman of her purse on a streetcar.
- November 1908 - Eddie Fitzgerald, robbery of a streetcar and occupants.
- November 1908 – Byron D. Wheelan alias Earl G. Westmore, robbery and evading police capture.
- July 1909 – J. Novak, murder.
- July 1909 – James Edward Cunningham, murder.

- September 1910 – Charles Brown, Charles Walters, William Smith arrested as a result of a raid on their gambling resort at Sixth and Stevenson streets.
- September 1910 – John Williams, arrested for illegal betting.
- September 1910 – Joseph Green, gambling resort proprietor, arrested.
- February 1911 – Thomas Shannon, robbery.
- March 1911 – Thomas Cosgrove, robbery.
- April 1911 – Fred Nefsky, robbery.
- August 1911 – James Trammell, fugitive.
- June 1912 – Chester Yates, fugitive from New York.
- March 1922 – George "Tony" Goursolle and Adrien Goursolle, robbery, home invasion, bootlegging.
- June 1923 – Clinton "Red" McCarthy, W.L. McMahon, E. O'Brien (alias John Murphy), James Stanley, Dave Collins, armed highway robbery.
- May 1926 – Julius and Ludwig Busch, bank robbery.
- January 1928 – Henry Rosenberg, altering checks.

bibliography

The story of Arthur McQuaide and his associates on both sides of the law falls within a relative gray area in law enforcement history. McQuaide's time had since surpassed that of the "Wild West" but not yet entered the decades defined by mob rule. Therefore, a variety of sources, both primary and secondary, were used to compile the information and context for this biography.

Unpublished Manuscripts and Letters

- *Trammell Family Papers and Correspondence*, Rector Public Library, Rector, Clay County, Arkansas.
- Steele, Harvey "That is Not Something You Need to Know': My Great-Grandfather Thomas Martin Anderson and the San Francisco Counterfeiting Adventure" (undated)

Articles and Essays

- Brand, Peter "The Killing of Charlie Storms by Luke Short: A Closer Look at the Gunfight and its Consequences" Wild West History Association *Journal* (March 2016)
- Monkkonen, Eric H. "A Disorderly People? Urban Order in the Nineteenth and Twentieth Centuries"

The Journal of American History Vol. 68, No. 3 (1981)
- Garnett, Porter (ed.) "Papers of the San Francisco Committee of Vigilance of 1851" *Academy of Pacific Coast History* Vol. 1, No. 7 (1910)
- Mullen, Kevin J. "Malachi Fallon, San Francisco's First Chief of Police" *California History* Vol. 62, No. 2 (1983)
- Key, V.O. Jr. "Police Graft" *American Journal of Sociology* Vol. 40, No. 5 (1935)
- Reynolds, C.N. "The Chinese Tongs" *American Journal of Sociology* Vol. 45, No. 5 (1935)
- Altrocchi, Julia Cooley "Paradox Town: San Francisco in 1851" *California Historical Society Quarterly* Vol. 28, No. 1 (1949)
- Garrett, Lula May "San Francisco in 1851 a Described by Eyewitnesses" *California Historical Society Quarterly* Vol. 22, No. 3 (1943)
- Rohrbough, Malcom "No Boy's Play: Migration and Settlement in Early Gold Rush California" *California History* Vol. 79 No. 2 (2000)
- Wright, Doris Marion "The Making of Cosmopolitan California: An Analysis of Immigration, 1848-1870" *California Historical Society Quarterly* Vol. 19, No. 4 (1940)
- Ricards, Sherman L. and Blackburn, George M. "They Sydney Ducks: A Demographic Analysis" *Pacific Historical Review* Vol. 42, No. 1 (1973)
- Campbell, Malcolm "Ireland's Furthest Shores: Irish Immigrant Settlement in Nineteenth-Century California and Eastern Australia" *Pacific Historical Review* Vol. 71. No. 1 (2002)

- Phelps, Robert "'All Hands Have Gone Downtown': Urban Spaces in Gold Rush California" *California History* Vol. 79, No. 2 (2000)
- Gay, Theressa "The California and Australia Gold Rushes: As Seen by Amos S. Pittman" *California Historical Society Quarterly* Vol. 30, No. 1 (1951)

Books

Asbury, Herbert. <u>The Barbary Coast: An Informal History of the San Francisco Underworld</u>. Basic Books, 2002.

Boessenecker, John <u>Gold Dust and Gunsmoke: Tales of Gold Rush Outlaws, Gunfighters, Lawmen, and Vigilantes</u>. John Wiley & Sons, Inc. 2000.

Dillon, Richard H. <u>The Hatchetmen: The Story of the Tong Wars in San Francisco's Chinatown</u>. Ballantine Books, 1972.

Emmons, David M. <u>Beyond the American Pale: The Irish in the American West, 1845-1910</u>. Norman: University of Oklahoma Press, 2010.

Fradkin, Philip L. <u>The Great Earthquake and Firestorms of 1906: How San Francisco Nearly Destroyed Itself</u>. Berkley: University of California Press, 2006.

Hughes, Robert <u>The Fatal Shore: The Epic of Australia's Founding</u>. Vintage Books, 1988.

Mullen, Kevin J. <u>Chinatown Squad: Policing the Dragon from the Gold Rush to the 21st Century</u>. Noir Publications, 2008.

- <u>The Toughest Gang in Town: Police Stories From Old San Francisco</u>. Noir Publications, 2005.

Smith, Dennis <u>San Francisco is Burning: The Untold Story of the 1906 Earthquake and Fires</u>. Plume, 2006.

Smyth, Terry <u>Australian Desperadoes: The Incredible Story of How Australian Gangsters Terrorized California</u>. Penguin Random House (Australia) 2018.

Walsh, James P. <u>The San Francisco Irish: 1850-1976</u>. The Executive of the Irish Literary and Historical Society 1979.

Wright, Erik J. <u>Main Street Mayhem: Crime, Murder & Justice in Downtown Paragould, 1888-1932</u>. Tripaw Press. 2016.

- <u>Gamblers, Guns & Gavels: Collected Works on Arizona Gambling Violence</u>. Tripaw Press, 2015.

Newspapers

Alta California

New York Times

Reno Gazette-Journal

San Francisco Call

San Francisco Chronicle

acknowledgements

This biography is the result of my research into the life and crimes of James Trammell of Arkansas and Australia. I began my investigations into that story around 2013 and it would not have been possible without the generous assistance of my longtime friend and fellow historian Peter Brand of Meadowbank, New South Wales, Australia. Furthermore, the living descendants of Trammell alive today in Australia are due a warm thank you.

Historians John Boessenecker and Casey Tefertiller, both of California's Bay Area have long provided ample information on that region's history. Samuel K. Dolan, author of *Cowboys and Gangsters: Stories of an Untamed Southwest* (2016), graciously agreed to pen the foreword to this book and my sincere thanks to him for doing so. I am also indebted to Mark Boardman, editor of the *National Tombstone Epitaph* for not only supporting my interest in Western history but nurturing my continued growth in the field.

Others who deserve thanks include the staff of the Greene County Public Library in Paragould, Arkansas for quickly and efficiently facilitating an obscure inter-library loan request to fulfill the research needs of this book; San Francisco Guardians of the City Museum and Memorial; Tom Carey, librarian and archivist at the San Francisco Public Library (San Francisco History Center).

My parents, Jeff and Kim Wright, who always encouraged my interests in history and never once denied me books deserve special thanks.

Additionally, my friends with the Paragould Police Department in Arkansas have helped me understand how modern policing works and by virtue of this I have gained a deeper appreciation for the job as well as the legacy of those who came before.

Lastly, my wife, Laura. A woman of sincere patience, caring, and understanding in any endeavor I undertake. Without whom no project would be possible -or worth-doing. I have all the love in the world for her and then some.

Erik Wright
Paragould, Arkansas

about the author

Erik J. Wright is the author of the dozens of papers and articles on crime, lawlessness, and warfare in the frontier west. He is a member of the Wild West History Association and the Pitcairn & Norfolk Islands Society. In 2017 he was elected as a member of the Royal Historical Society. Wright serves as assistant editor of the *National Tombstone Epitaph* and has authored three books. He works as the coordinator of the Greene County Office of Emergency Management in northeast Arkansas where he lives with his wife, Laura and their three dogs.

also by the author

Nonfiction

Gamblers, Guns, and Gavels: Collected Works on Arizona Gambling Violence

Main Street Mayhem: Crime, Murder, and Justice in Downtown Paragould, 1888-1932

Phil Foote: Lawman, Outlaw… Hell-Raiser

Selected Papers

The Top & Bottom Gang in Arizona: A Documentary History

Thomas Mulqueen: Two-Fisted Gambler

Fresh Light on the Death of Highwayman Bill Brazelton: A Critical Review of Secondary Sources

David Gibson: Boy-Soldier, Gambler, Man-Killer

Johnny Murphy: Irish Gambler on the Arizona Frontier

Leo Schmucker: Lawman in the Transitional West and the Lewis Reynolds Killers

Made in the USA
Columbia, SC
12 October 2018